Order this book online at www.trafford.com/08-0894
or email orders@trafford.com

Most Trafford titles are also available at major online book retailers.

© Copyright 2008 Metropolitan Community Churches.
Compiled by Rev. Dr. Cindi H. Love, Edited by Leah Sloan
Cover Design by Joseph Rattan, Plano TX (www.josephrattandesigns.com)
Design by Rev. Dr. Cindi H. Love and Joseph Rattan

Note for Librarians: A cataloguing record for this book is available from Library
and Archives Canada at www.collectionscanada.ca/amicus/index-e.html

Printed in Victoria, BC, Canada.

ISBN: 978-1-4251-8283-0

*We at Trafford believe that it is the responsibility of us all, as both individuals and corporations,
to make choices that are environmentally and socially sound. You, in turn, are supporting this
responsible conduct each time you purchase a Trafford book, or make use of our publishing services.
To find out how you are helping, please visit www.trafford.com/responsiblepublishing.html*

*Our mission is to efficiently provide the world's finest, most comprehensive book publishing
service, enabling every author to experience success. To find out how to publish your book, your
way, and have it available worldwide, visit us online at www.trafford.com/10510*

Trafford
PUBLISHING® www.trafford.com

North America & international
toll-free: 1 888 232 4444 (USA & Canada)
phone: 250 383 6864 ♦ fax: 250 383 6804 ♦ email: info@trafford.com

The United Kingdom & Europe
phone: +44 (0)1865 487 395 ♦ local rate: 0845 230 9601
facsimile: +44 (0)1865 481 507 ♦ email: info.uk@trafford.com

10 9 8 7 6 5 4 3 2

40 YEARS

Of Faith, Hope and Love.

Metropolitan Community Churches

WE ARE THE CHURCH ALIVE

We are the Church Alive, Christ's presence on this earth;
We give God's Spirit body in the act of our new birth.
As yielded open channels for God's descending dove,
We shout and sing, with joy we bring God's all inclusive love.

We are the Church Alive, Our faith has set us free;
No more enslaved by guilt and shame, we live our liberty!
We follow Christ's example and freedom now proclaim,
Destroying myths of doubt and fear in Jesus' mighty name.

We are the Church Alive, The body must be healed;
Where strife has bruised and battered us, God's wholeness is revealed.
Our mission is an urgent one; In strength and health let's stand,
So that our witness to God's light will shine in ev'ry land.

We are the Church Alive, All praise to God on high.
Creator, Savior, Comforter! We laud and magnify
Your name, Almighty God of love; Pray give us life that we
May be your Church, the Church Alive, For all eternity.

Text:
Jack Hoggatt-St. John
and David Pelletier,
1980

Music:
Jack Hoggatt-St. John,
1980

Copyright © 1980
Jack Hoggatt-St. John
and David Pelletier.

The hymn, "The Church
Alive" was written
for the Fifth Anniversary
Celebration of the
Metropolitan Community Church
of the Willamette Valley
in Eugene, OR.

MUSIC | "WE ARE THE CHURCH ALIVE"
JACK HOGGATT-ST. JOHN & DAVID PELLETIER ©1980 | MCC SAN FRANCISCO HYMNAL #176

BUILT ON HOPE

We are united, a family of faith,
Impassioned for justice and humbled by grace,
Following with fervor the One who led us here,
Who will give us joy for sorrow and offers hope for fear.
(Chorus)

We have decided to follow this Christ,
Who overthrows injustice, who offers new life,
Who fed all the hungry and healed all who hurt,
If you're looking for our faith, may you find it in our works.
(Chorus)

A hope of peace and freedom, of faith and harmony,
What if it's up to you and me???

(Chorus)
Hope that works, Hope that tries,
Hope that sees Christ in their eyes,
Hope that heals and won't tear down,
Hope that's built on solid ground.
You have given us this mission so we know,
We can create a world of faith that's built on hope.

Text:
Marsha Stevens-Pino

Music:
Marsha Stevens-Pino

Copyright © 2007
Balm Ministries (ASCAP)

The song, "Built On Hope"
is the most recent
anthem written for Metropolitan
Community Churches and
was sung at MCC's 2007 General
Conference in Scottsdale, AZ.

"I spent 1980 in Eugene, Oregon, working with David Pelletier at MCC of the Willamette Valley as Minister of Music. In those days there were some significant themes that resonated through the Gay and Lesbian community and specifically in MCC: freedom from guilt and shame, destroying myths of doubt and fear, and the need to heal divisions within Christianity as it struggled with homophobia and sexism. These became embedded within the overall theme that we are the church, that our aliveness is what gives the church its life, and that we have a mission to spread God's love in the world.

We can thank David for the trinitarian language in the final verse, and have been gratified and blessed that so many people have sung and loved our hymn over the years."

Jack Hoggatt

For 40 years MCC has offered the Gospel, the "Good News," to a community wounded by homophobia and religious bigotry, and hungry for something other than "bad news" from the Church.

IN 1968, BEFORE THE STONEWALL REBELLION, Troy Perry placed an ad in *The Advocate* inviting homosexuals, and any other brave souls who were interested, to a worship service in his home in Huntington Park, California (USA). At the time, homosexuality was a crime, a diagnosable mental illness and a sin so grave that few but the most fanatical ever spoke of it publicly. In several states homosexuals could not assemble publicly without being in violation of the law, and some jurisdictions required that homosexuals be registered as sex offenders with local law enforcement.

Although a few secretive organizations and a handful of people had begun to work toward civil rights for homosexuals, the general public was largely unaware of those efforts and intolerant of non-heterosexuality. Rev. Perry says he organized the service in his home because there was no other safe, welcoming place for him to meet with other people and worship God. He says he had no idea that one small gathering would initiate a church movement that would rock the Church, the nation and the world; sweeping across 25 countries, inspiring the "open and affirming movement," and kicking off an interfaith explosion of LGBT religious movements.

Metropolitan Community Church on the corner of
22nd Street and Union Street in Los Angeles, California.

A portrait of Rev. Troy Perry.

Rev. Troy Perry, Rev. June Norris and Rev. Lee Spangenberg lead
evening worship at the Help Center. Worship took place here
after a fire destroyed the Mother Church at 22nd & Union in Los Angeles.

"I had no idea that one small gathering would initiate a church movement that would rock the Church, the nation and the world; sweeping across 25 countries, inspiring the 'open and affirming movement,' and kicking off an interfaith explosion of LGBT religious movements."   *Rev. Troy Perry*

Rev. Jide Macaulay of MCC North London, who ministers at House of Rainbow, Lagos, Nigeria, with Rev. Elder Troy Perry at the People of African Descent (PAD) Conference in 2008.

FROM THAT FIRST WORSHIP SERVICE, Rev. Perry's (and ultimately MCC's) message has been effectively strong, simple and inclusive; and the three-pronged gospel he preached—salvation, community, and Christian social action—still functions as the core of the mission and values statement of MCC Worldwide.

In the earliest years, someone urged Troy Perry to use more than just his Pentecostal background in creating a welcome for all people, and to form instead a grassroots, ecumenical expression of church. Guided by God and using the strength of his own personality, boundless energy and relentless optimism, that's exactly what Rev. Perry did. From the beginning, Metropolitan Community Church has offered an open table for communion with no barriers to any person of any faith tradition. In addition, Troy Perry determined in 1968, that he would marry same-sex couples as a sacrament and an act of non-violent protest of discrimination against our community. He filed the first lawsuit for recognition of those marriages in the United States. His decision to lead MCC as a justice-seeking church preaching an all-inclusive gospel has been the refiner's fire of our movement. Our ministry has grown and has been sustained through some incredibly difficult and challenging times, and 40 years later, Metropolitan Community Churches continues to carry God's message of love and inclusion to the world.

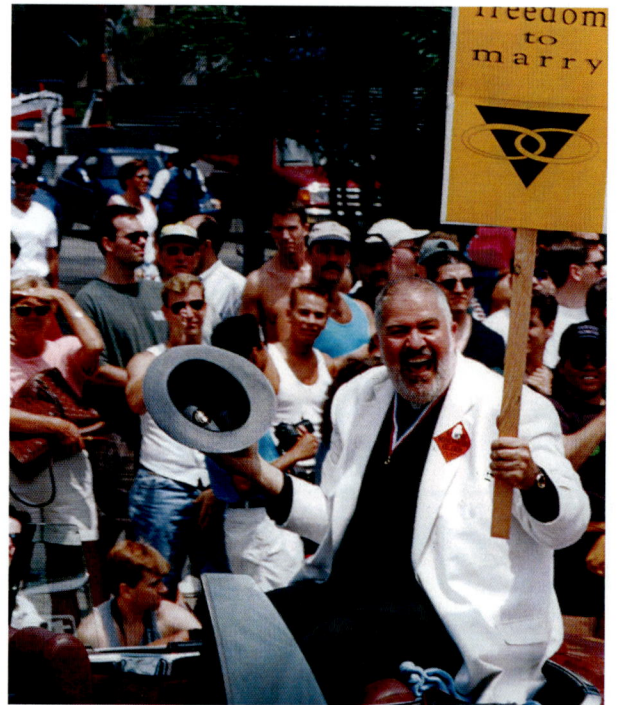

(at left) Rev. Troy Perry gathers with others on the corner of Hollywood Boulevard & Las Palmas in the Heart of Hollywood.

(above) Rev. Elder Troy Perry rides in the Los Angeles Gay Pride Parade in the late 1990s and speaks out for the freedom of same-sex couples to marry.

(at right) Rev. Troy Perry and MCC-LA host Los Angeles mayor Tom Bradley during morning worship.

"Rev. Perry's decision to lead MCC as a justice-seeking church preaching an all-inclusive gospel has been the 'refiner's fire' of our movement."

MCC

VALUES

&VISION

Transforming Hearts, Lives and History.

Metropolitan Community Churches

Metropolitan Community Churches are on a bold mission to transform hearts, lives, and history. We are a movement that faithfully proclaims God's inclusive love for all people and proudly bears witness to the holy integration of spirituality and sexuality.

Because of our faith we are called to:

do justice, show kindness, and live humbly with God. (Micah 6:8)

explore life's questions with open hearts and minds.

raise our voices in sacred defiance against exclusion, whether religious, political or systemic.

reach out to those with no hope.

equip new generations of remarkable, far-reaching spiritual activists.

HERE'S TO THE NEXT 40 YEARS!

In contemplating MCC's 40th anniversary I've been both reflecting on the many changes I've seen in my 36 years of involvement, and daring to imagine the challenging path before us. At 40 years, we, like the Israelites wandering in the wilderness, haven't quite reached the land of milk and honey, but even though I expect there's still a bit more wilderness to pass through, I'm confident we will reach the Promised Land.

My best hope is that in 2048 MCC will be widely known as a trustworthy movement of God, still passionate about justice and the inclusive gospel of Jesus Christ. I believe that we will:

Moderator Rev. Elder Nancy Wilson

1. still be preaching that God loves all people and that it is possible to be Christian regardless of sexuality, orientation or gender identification.
2. comprehend sexuality and gender as fluid, multi-dimensional constructs and have a better understanding of our bodies, health, and addiction.
3. be Christians preaching an open, progressive message of acceptance and freedom in an increasingly pluralistic world, and honoring all positive spiritual paths.
4. be about God's mission of justice, peace, and hope; going wherever in the world there is need to "tear down walls and build up hope."
5. be living among communities hungry for an authentic spiritual talk and walk—whether the problems of extreme poverty, population growth, climate destabilization, and human rights have been adequately addressed or not, people will need us.
6. be working with a network of spiritual and secular partners, all of us equally committed to changing the world.
7. seldom be all together as one Body, but will worship together and be in community with each other using as-yet unimagined technology.
8. be dealing with the positive and negative effects of globalization, as well as experiencing the growing influence and leadership of the South and the East.

I cannot speculate as to when or where MCC's Moderator in 2048 will have been born, and I can only wonder whether any of the stories told at General Conference then will be about our previous and current struggles for dignity, equality and human rights. Will they remember our prayers and our tears, the times we celebrated success and the times we vowed to fight on?

I can say though that I'll be with you, MCC—if not in the flesh (at age 98!) then in spirit—cheering you on with a host of others, thrilled to have made a difference with an amazing community blessed by the Holy Spirit of God.

Grace and Peace,

Nancy Wilson

DEAR SAINTS

What a marvelous time for Metropolitan Community Churches! Little did we know on October 6, 1968 that 40 years later there would be Metropolitan Community Churches world-wide, proclaiming the Good News of Jesus' love for all of us.

It has not always been an easy journey. During those early years, twenty-one of our churches were either desecrated or burned. Over the 40-year period, five of our clergy have been murdered. Yet through all of that, our Church has kept the faith knowing that God loves us and that our message and its proclamation were too important to let anything stop us. I believe God said I was to proclaim the three-pronged Gospel of Christian Salvation, Christian Community and Christian Social Action to the gay, lesbian, bisexual and transgender community and all others who would hear it, and we have kept to that message. While there was sometimes sorrow, there was lots of joy in our Church. It was the joy of our salvation that got us through rough times.

Rev. Elder Troy Perry

Had you told me in October of 1968 that in 40 years we and God's revelation to us would have helped change the world, I'm not sure I would have believed you. In fact, many people said it was impossible, but we did it!

As I approach the 40th anniversary of the founding of our movement, I can only look forward to the joy that I know God has in the future for us. My greatest hope and dream for the next generation of our membership and our leadership is that our Church will continue to be on the cutting edge of carrying the Gospel of Jesus Christ into all the world. So many people across the globe still live where they have no justice, no liberties and no freedoms simply because of who they are. It is the responsibility of this Church to remember that God has called us to be faithful and fearless!

In Christ,

Rev. Elder Troy D. Perry
Founder

DEAR FRIENDS AND FAMILY OF
METROPOLITAN COMMUNITY CHURCH

I want to begin this letter by expressing my deep appreciation for you. The truth for MCC is that our ministry and movement would not be experiencing this 40th anniversary without your contributions and those of the many who have gone before us. Thank you.

It has been an honor and privilege to work with the 40th Anniversary Team on this publication, *Forty Years of Faith, Hope & Love*, and on the oral history and archives project, *In Our Own Words* (www.InOurOwnWordsMCC.org)

I think you can imagine the laughter and tears shared among the team as those over age 55 tried to explain MCC to those not yet 25. Questions like "Now, who was Anita Bryant?" proved to be quite revealing and affirmed our decision to include historically focused projects in the celebration of the 40th Anniversary.

Executive Director, Rev. Dr. Cindi Love

This publication groups the years 1968 to 2008 into five sections:

- Formation
- Development
- Tribulation
- Human Rights
- Renewal

A timeline reflecting these subdivisions progresses throughout the publication and includes significant events in MCC history along with photos and images from each period.

The narrative provides the global historical context within which our ministry and movement was evolving and relates events that were "tipping points" for MCC's internal development. For example, Rev. Jim Sandmire's sermon, delivered to the third General Conference in Los Angeles at a time Rev. Elder Troy Perry described as a crossroads for MCC, is featured on Page 23.

There was no way to include everyone or everything that can be considered significant in the history of MCC. We do hope, though, that reviewing the highlights will spark further interest and that you will share your story at www.InOurOwnWordsMCC.org so future generations can appreciate the richness and complexity of the MCC experience.

I want to acknowledge and thank Joe Rattan, Angel Collie, Rev. Karla Fleshman, Melanie Martinez, Leah Sloan, Frank Zerilli, Franklin Calvin, Adrain Bowie-Mobley and Carlos Chavez for their incredible collaboration and commitment to the 40th Anniversary publication and oral history project.

My prayer is that this publication will touch your heart and spirit in the way that its compilation did mine. I am a relative newcomer to MCC and the process of reviewing our history and listening to your stories "shook my foundations" in a very positive way. The commitment I held for MCC was strengthened yet again by your witness.

Thank you!

Blessings and Peace,

Cynthia H. Love, Ed.D

Rev. Dr. Cindi Love
Executive Director

DEAR MCC FRIENDS

As we mark our 40th Anniversary, we are now well into our effort to restructure Fellowship operations to position ourselves for an even greater future. One of our bold restructuring initiatives was to create of a Board of Administration with a mandate to focus like a laser beam on financial and "business" operations—ensuring maximum efficiency and effectiveness. In Biblical terms, this is called "good stewardship."

With expert guidance from our Executive Director, and enthusiastic support from the Moderator and Board of Elders, the "business" side of MCC is making dramatic leaps forward, building momentum for the future. Here are just a few things we can celebrate:

Rev. Jeff Miner

■ Despite great budgetary pressure, the planned reduction of mandated tithes and assessments on local churches has been honored. Further, many churches have begun voluntarily contributing more than what is mandated – in beautiful acts of generosity that are enabling our worldwide work to move forward.

■ Our senior spiritual leaders – the Elders – are operating as a cohesive team, sharing expertise and support regardless of regional boundaries, thereby promoting maximum efficiency. We are one in Christ.

■ An awesome, experienced Fund Development Director was hired just this year to coordinate Fellowship-wide efforts to expand our funding base.

■ MCC's most valuable fixed asset, the headquarters building in Los Angeles, was sold at the peak of the real estate market, liquidating virtually all MCC debts and allowing the development of investment accounts that will generate a continuous revenue stream for MCC operations in the years ahead.

■ A visionary project to develop an LGBT-friendly, MCC-affiliated senior housing community is well underway, with exciting developments just around the corner. This project too will generate revenue for MCC operations in the future.

We give thanks to God for all of this and more – and for MCCers everywhere whose support and trust have made this stewardship progress possible. We live in an increasingly globalized, web-based world that changes at the speed of light. In this brave new world, organizations that are open, flexible, and willing to adapt continuously will prosper, while those resistant to progress will wither. I want to encourage us all, as a matter of faithful stewardship, to remain open and flexible and to allow the Holy Spirit to mold us into an ever-more-powerful force for good in this world.

In Christ,

Rev. Jeff Miner
Chair, Board of Administration

ON OCTOBER 6, 1968 AT 1:30 P.M., TWELVE PEOPLE GATHERED with Rev. Troy Perry in his home in Huntington Park, California for the first worship service of what has become Metropolitan Community Church worldwide.

In reality, that inaugural assembly was also an act of non-violent protest in opposition to religious bigotry which had led to endemic discrimination against lesbian, gay, bisexual, transgender and intersex people. From that first meeting, the people of MCC have been on a pilgrimage toward true self—the sort of journey that May Sarton wrote [takes] "Time, many years and places." Certainly this has been the experience of MCC as our people have carried our message of hope and healing to 25 countries and hundreds of cities, while wrestling with the challenges of inclusive language and gender bias, racism, classism, HIV/AIDS and patriarchy.

Sarton said the world needs people with the patience and the passion to make this kind of pilgrimage not only for their own sakes, but also as social and political acts [because] the world still waits for the truth that will set us all free—my truth, your truth, our truth—the truth that was seeded in the earth when we were formed here in the image of God.

This pilgrimage has not been a path of least resistance for our people; it has not been a path

Rev. Troy Perry and Steve Jordan mix paint for the Metropolitan Community Church Parish House.

In the summer of 1968, one year prior to the Stonewall events, a little-reported West Coast bar action and police confrontation serves to galvanize gay activists in Los Angeles, CA (USA). The chain of events which will lead directly to the founding of the first Metropolitan Community Church is initiated.

Troy Perry holds the first worship service of what would come to be known as MCC-Los Angeles. Twelve worshipers gathered in his home in Huntington Park, CA at 1:30 p.m. on October 6, 1968.

On December 3, 1968, the nation's first same-sex marriage is performed by Rev. Troy Perry for two Mexican-American men in Los Angeles, CA.

1968

Formation Years

MCC's first seven years included incorporation, the first General Conference, the first gay/lesbian pride parade, acquisition of the first property owned by an LGBT organization in the United States, ordination of the first woman and tragic loss of the Mother Church to fire.

October 6, 1968—the date of the first service of what today has become an international movement with more than 44,000 members and adherents in 25 countries, an annual income exceeding $26 million, and a powerful message of spiritual acceptance and affirmation for gays, lesbians, bisexuals and transgendered persons.

without tribulation. It has been instead a path of patience, persistence and faithful application of the core values stated by Rev. Troy Perry: community, justice and salvation. He and hundreds of faithful followers have raised up a generation of far-reaching spiritual activists—indeed the type of cohort Bayard Rustin must have meant when he referred to "a group of angelic troublemakers"—who have literally changed the world. Rev. Perry stepped out in faith in a time of global transformation, a time in which people who had never before "acted up" were challenging the values of their families and churches and communities and countries.

It was the perfect time for the birth of MCC.

And what was happening during this formation period? During the first two years of MCC's existence, the Supreme Court heard the case of students at North High School in Des Moines, Iowa, who had been suspended for mourning the dead in Vietnam by wearing peace symbol-adorned black armbands. In West Berlin 10,000 people demonstrated against the war in Vietnam, and the United States sent 10,500 additional soldiers to the war. Robert F. Kennedy and Rev. Martin Luther King, Jr. were both assassinated. Pope Paul VI published *Humanae Vitae* which prohibited the faithful from using artificial forms of birth control. There were race riots in Chicago,

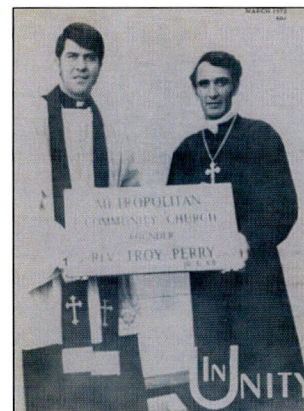

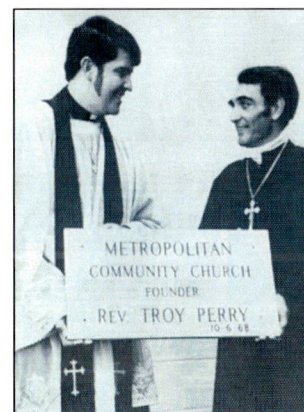

On the cover and interior of *In Unity* Magazine, Rev. Troy Perry and Deacon Fred Sferrazzo with the cornerstone of the Mother Church. It commemorates the date of the first service of an MCC congregation and was presented to Rev. Perry by MCC-LA at the third anniversary dinner.

The first Christopher Street Gay Pride Parade in New York City on the anniversary of the Stonewall riots.

Metropolitan Community Church congregations are formed in nine cities in the USA: Los Angeles, San Francisco, San Diego and Costa Mesa, CA; Chicago, IL; Phoenix, AZ; Kaneone, HI; Dallas, TX and Miami, FL.

Rev. Perry leads a group of demonstrators to the Dover Hotel in Los Angeles, CA to protest the beating death of a young gay man by local police officers.

1969

UFMCC's commitment to Christian Social Action is tested in April 1969, when Rev. Perry leads a group of eight MCC-LA members in a peaceful demonstration in front of the Los Angeles offices of State Steamship Lines, which had fired a man for publicly declaring his homosexuality.

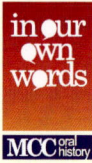

Intermittently placed throughout this publication you'll find selected quotes—most of them from long-time MCC members—highlighted in colorful sidebars. The quotes are excerpts from *In Our Own Words MCC*, the program title for MCC's Archive and Oral History Project.

The project is designed to capture, gather and share individuals' recollections and thoughts about important events in MCC's history as a movement, ministry and community. The project is extensive, long-term and ongoing—the past will always hold the key to the future, but its value can be optimized only by open and honest consideration. We must record and remember our successes; we must also document and reflect on the things that didn't work so well lest we risk repeated mistakes.

At www.InOurOwnWordsMCC.org you can see videos, hear oral histories, read transcripts, and connect with the people of MCC through the richness of their personal accounts. You can also participate in the project by sharing your own experiences. After all, in forty years, the things we're doing now will have been incorporated into the MCC legacy and the next generation will be intensely interested.

Miami and Little Rock. *Funny Girl* with Barbra Streisand premiered. Arthur Ashe was the first person of color to be ranked #1 in tennis and Billie Jean King beat Dr. Vija Vuskanis in the first stadium match at the US Open. On December 3, 1968, Rev. Troy Perry performed the nation's first same-sex marriage and shortly afterwards filed the first lawsuit to recognize such marriages in the United States. In 1969, Rev. Perry led a group of demonstrators to the Dover Hotel in Los Angeles, CA to protest local police having beaten a young gay man who subsequently died.

Within a few short years, Rev. Troy Perry and a rapidly growing group of MCC members and friends effectively called the question to the Church Universal, "Can a person be Christian and gay?" Simultaneously, they not only insisted that homosexuals had a civil right to marriage, but also demanded the rights to protection from hate crimes and equal protection under the law with regard to employment and housing.

In 1970, Rev. Perry helped organize the first Gay/Lesbian Pride Parade in LA. After the march, Perry, joined by representatives from the Daughters of Bilitis and the Homophile Effort for Legal Protection, sat at a busy street corner in Hollywood, California and began a fast to bring about meaningful dialogue on changing unjust laws that discriminated against lesbians and gay men.

Rev. Perry helps organize and marches in Los Angeles' first Gay/Lesbian Pride Parade. After the March, Rev. Perry, joined by representatives from Daughters of Bilitis and the Homophile Effort for Legal Protection, begins a public fast in order to encourage meaningful dialogue about changing unjust laws that discriminate against lesbians and gay men.

At the first General Conference of UFMCC, more than 600 people attend Sunday morning worship. The group of MCC churches in the USA agree to form a body they will call the Universal Fellowship of Metropolitan Community Churches and agree to begin development of an educational institution, Samaritan Institute for Religious Studies. Rev. Dr. Mona West (pictured at left) served as Dean. The school trained clergy for MCC from 1993 to 1997.

1970

General Conference I September 1970 Los Angeles, California
Held on borrowed property in and around the city of Los Angeles.
Churches & Missions represented:
Los Angeles, San Diego, San Francisco, Chicago, Phoenix, Hawaii, Costa Mesa and Dallas.
First Board of Elders elected: Rev. Troy Perry, Rev. John Hose, Rev. Richard Ploen and Rev. Louis Loynes.

Metropolitan Community Church establishes the "Mother Church" with the purchase of the property on the corner of 22nd Street and Union Street in L.A. The detail at right is of the beautiful stained glass window there.

The Rite of Holy Union is added to UFMCC Bylaws.

MCC Los Angeles ("Mother Church") becomes the first gay/lesbian organization in the USA to own its own property with the purchase and renovation of a church at 22nd St and Union St. in Los Angeles.

Rev. Elder Troy Perry leads a march from San Francisco to the California state capitol at Sacramento to demand support for a Consenting Adults Bill.

1971

General Conference II September 1971 Los Angeles, California
Guest speaker: Dr. Evelyn Hooker, Chairperson of the Task Force on Homosexuality for the National Institute of Mental Health, by the appointment of President Lyndon B. Johnson
Churches & Missions represented:
Los Angeles, San Diego, San Francisco, Phoenix, Hawaii, Chicago, Costa Mesa, Dallas, Oakland, Sacramento, San Jose, Fresno, Denver, Tucson, Milwaukee, New Orleans, Tampa, Miami, Washington, DC.

IT TOOK REAL COURAGE to take this type of public stand in such a divided society—recall that anyone with long hair or wearing a peace symbol was regarded as enemy by "the establishment" and protest actions were often disrupted by the use of physical violence. Rev. Troy and his allies began their fast the month after four students in an anti-war demonstration at Kent State were killed by Ohio National Guardsmen.

From 1972 until 1983, Metropolitan Community Church became an increasingly complex organization and also experienced tremendous growth in membership, number of locations and worldwide influence. Following UFMCC's California incorporation in 1970, the thirty-five congregations that had emerged during the formative years multiplied rapidly throughout the United States. In July 1972, Rev. Perry led his people in what became a standard practice of engaging major national and international political figures, both pro- and anti-gay, in dialogue about human rights. MCC's first direct action occurred at the Democratic National Convention at the Deauville Hotel in Miami; their goal was to achieve an audience with presidential nominee George McGovern, who was an early and vocal opponent of US military involvement in Vietnam.

At General Conference III in September 1972, MCC voted to establish itself as a permanent denomination. Soon thereafter,

Rev. Howard Wells, Founding Pastor of MCC San Francisco.

(below top) Jo McVay-Abbott, Birmingham U.K.
Freda Smith, Executive Secretary of World Church Extension
and Jose Von Buhler, Thames Valley U.K.
(below bottom, l to r) MCC in Auckland NZ: Richard Warnock,
Rev. Leigh Neighbour, Bill Hein and David A. Taggert.

In July, UFMCC participates in an action at the Democratic National Convention at the Deauville Hotel in Miami, hoping to achieve an audience with presidential nominee George McGovern.

The National Prison Ministry is established to provide ministry and counseling for the imprisoned and parole support for those being released. The program was renamed the Board of Institutional Ministry in 1975 and the Office of Institutional Ministry in 1979.

1972

Growth Years

As MCC grows, global outreach begins. The first application to the National Council of Churches is made. The first trans-person and the first African-American are licensed as clergy. MCC leads the fight against the Briggs Initiative and prevails. The Committee on Lay Concerns is formed.

General Conference III September 1972 Los Angeles, California Convenes with representatives from 35 congregations. MCC votes to establish itself as a permanent denomination. California State Assemblyman Willie Brown, who has sponsored the Consenting Adults Law in the California Assembly, is the guest speaker. The list of cities represented lengthens to include Riverside, Santa Barbara, Venice, Long Beach, San Fernando Valley, Colorado Springs, Fort Lauderdale, Atlanta, Boston, Detroit, New York, Philadelphia, Nashville, Austin, Seattle, and Salt Lake City.

this new denomination "went global" establishing MCC congregations in London, England (UK) and Toronto, Ontario (Canada), and accepting invitations to visit in Australia and Nigeria as well. It is again important to take note of the broader social context in which globalization was occurring. The leap of faith that carried MCC outside the borders of the US ran parallel to the social movement of Greenpeace, "an independent, campaigning organization which used peaceful direct action and creative communication to expose global environmental problems and to force solutions for a green and peaceful future." This leap of faith frightened many conservative and "closeted" members of MCC.

The church which had grown so vitally from its infancy was suddenly operating on a world stage, and some conservative members, unsure about MCC's involvement with Christian liberation theology, struggled for a retreat toward social invisibility. Rev. Perry said later in his book *Don't Be Afraid Anymore* that they feared Rev. Perry's leading MCC into participation in vocal and/or visible gay community action; they believed that MCC had done enough to promote public enlightenment. Rev. Perry, on the other hand, believed that MCC was, like the early Christian Church, required by God to engage in social action.

It may seem peculiar to say that during the first two years of MCC, when the people met to pray, were derided and evicted, and were forced to move from one place to another, they were unknowingly experiencing the easiest years of MCC's existence. Somewhere along the way, a significant number

Our faith is tested by fire: In January, the sanctuary of MCC Los Angeles is destroyed; in March, a fire is set at MCC Nashville in Tennessee; and in June, an arsonist's fire in the French Quarter destroys a bar once used as a meeting place for MCC New Orleans. At least 29 people die, including local MCC Pastor, Rev. William Larson.

UFMCC begins its Global Outreach with the establishment of MCC of London in England (United Kingdom) and MCC of Toronto in Ontario, Canada.

UFMCC's Bylaws are rewritten to be less gender-specific and more inclusive.

1973

Rev. Freda Smith becomes the first woman ordained as clergy in UFMCC and the first woman elected to the UFMCC Board of Elders. Rev. June Norris is the first heterosexual person to be licensed as clergy in UFMCC.

General Conference IV August/September 1973 Atlanta, Georgia
Theme: Onward—As One
Bylaw revision includes expanding the Board of Elders;
Rev. Troy Perry, Rev. John Hose, Rev. Richard Ploen, Rev. John Gill,
Rev. Richard Vincent, Rev. Freda Smith, and Rev. Jim Sandmire elected.

I love, I absolutely love the ministry of MCC. I believe we're the new Reformation of the Christian Church. I believe that we have… made an enormous contribution: women in ministry, inclusive language, social action …incredible!

But we have much farther to go so…we are the new Reformation of the Christian Church. And the most exciting church since the Book of Acts!

…I was…ordained and elected to the Board of Elders in 1973…and at that Conference all of the bylaws had only male language. Actually the ministers were all male—the deacons, the exhorters—the bylaws used "he" all the way through.

At the 1973 conference was where I stood up and made the motion, all the way through, to change the 'he's to 'he's and 'she's so that there wasn't any office in Metropolitan Community Church that could possibly be closed to women. And that was the very first inclusive language we did was 1973 in the Bylaws.

Rev. Elder Freda Smith,
Sutter Creek, California, USA

of MCC insiders had developed the mindset that the Church's only reason for being was to encourage long-established denominations to reexamine their homophobic theological interpretations. Many members agreed that once the extent of hypocrisy in other churches was revealed, their unchristian attitudes would surely be corrected and—extending that overly optimistic theory—that each MCC member would be then be warmly welcomed back into the reformed denomination of his or her original persuasion. Rev. Troy Perry said, "Many of us who should have known better commented more than once, 'We are working ourselves out of business.'"

Soul-wrenching questions shook us to our core: Was it proper for MCC to cease to exist when—if—other denominations eventually accepted homosexuals as God's children? Or, was it God's intention that UFMCC should remain visible and continue to grow? There was no consensus amongst members of MCC. In 1972 Rev. Jim Sandmire preached at General Conference III in Los Angeles—the crossroads of the MCC experience. He said,

Metropolitan Community Church, Los Angeles

In January, the chapel owned by the non-denominational Unity-by-the-Sea Church and rented by West Bay MCC Santa Monica, CA, suffers $20,000 in damage from another arson-induced blaze.

The Mother Church purchases the old Belasco Theater in downtown Los Angeles to serve as their new home. The historic building on Hill Street will also house the UFMCC offices.

UFMCC representatives visit groups in Australia and Nigeria. Congregations form in Adelaide, Melbourne and Sydney, Australia. In Nigeria, Rev. Sylvanus Maduka becomes the first licensed UFMCC clergyperson from outside the United States. Rev. Maduka and Rev. Jose Mojica are the first persons of color to be licensed as clergy.

1974

General Conference V August 1974 San Francisco, California
Theme: One Body, One Lord, One Faith, One Baptism
Conference votes to begin the application process for National Council of Churches and World Council of Churches memberships.
Rev. Roy Birchard elected to the Board of Elders.

"DISSOLUTION OF MCC UNDER ANY CIRCUMSTANCE WOULD BE A TERRIBLE TRAGEDY, particularly if God has truly called us to be an authentic voice of our time. I believe we are the new establishment church. I believe we are a new expression of the Gospel. I believe God has called us to be a guide for other churches which need to be shown the way toward a rediscovery of Jesus' love. But, I fear we have allowed ourselves to become complacent... My concern is that although most of us are gay, we are in danger of becoming a pale reprint of all the self-righteous, do-nothing churches we came from. The irony is that as we seem to become less active in pursuit of gay and lesbian rights, several of the denominations we fled years ago seem finally to be responding to renewal, ... Therefore, if the Fellowship is to continue as a meaningful religious experience, we need to make these essential assumptions: our theology needs to remain basic, centered on the love of God with genuine expressions of goodness and responsibility to others. An example...was set nearly two thousand years ago by Jesus—who consorted with outcasts, championed the weak and raised the humble...I urge an end to middle-class introversion and the beginning of opening the Fellowship to more young people, to more heterosexuals, more minority groups and a lot more on the distaff side. I believe God would desire that we stop talking about going out of business and start actually being the new prophetic voice to the world. A church like Metropolitan Community Church has never before existed anywhere on earth. If it is God's will that Metropolitan Community Church shall continue to grow and go forward, then all gifts of the Holy Spirit that identify the church will be ours. Amen."

(clockwise from left)
Rev. Lee Carlton, Rev. Don Pederson,
Rev. Bud Bunce, Rev. Tom Bigelow, Rev. Paul Van Hecke,
Rev. Willie Smith and Rev. June Norris.

The General Conference votes unanimously to recommend that every member church begin working toward the use of inclusive language.

In October, UFMCC opens a Field Office in Washington, DC to initiate and lobby for social action.

Rev. Elder Jim Sandmire

1975

Rev. Heather Anderson (now Rev. Sky Anderson) is the first transgendered person licensed as clergy in UFMCC.

General Conference VI July/August 1975 Dallas, Texas
Theme: We've A Story To Tell To The Nations
Guest speakers included Rev. Dr. Norman Pittinger, clergyman, author & theologian; and
Elaine Noble, Massachusetts State Representative.
Rev. Carol Cureton elected to the Board of Elders.

AIDS consumed us...We buried, in the ten years between 1984 and 1994/95, over 400 people who sat in our pews at MCC of the Rockies. The congregation was 300, 315, thereabouts during that timeframe, and we buried over 400 who used to sit in those pews...I would say from 1991 until I left in August of '95, it was not unusual to have from one to three or four memorial services a week...

The great failure for me was, I was so busy making hospital calls and planning the next funeral...we didn't have time to do any follow-up whatsoever with everybody who had lost people... I commented to the President of the Iowa School of Theology... one day... "Don, I feel like I'm a rabbi in Auschwitz, not a pastor of a modern church in the United States."

...AIDS consumed us. I dealt with death and dying constantly...it was the life of the parish. Oh yes, we had parties, we had this we had that...but death was...was...was life! That's the way it was.

Rev. Elder Charlie Arehart,
Las Vegas, Nevada, USA

When Rev. Sandmire stopped preaching, Rev. Troy Perry opened up his Bible and reread the list of spiritual gifts—wisdom, knowledge, faith, gifts of healing, working of miracles, prophecy, discerning of spirits, diverse tongues, interpretation of tongues. He says the rest of the service that evening was profoundly moving and he searched his soul for the next steps he should take in leading the people of MCC. The die was cast.

Shortly thereafter, the Equal Rights Amendment was at the forefront of American politics, and in 1973 MCC ordained its first female clergy member, Rev. Freda Smith, and also elected her to the Board of Elders. That same year, Rev. June Norris was the first heterosexual person to be licensed as MCC clergy and MCC's bylaws were rewritten to be less gender-specific and more inclusive.

(from l to r) Rev. Troy Perry, Rev. Jose Mojica and another Pastor lead a Metropolitan Community Church worship service in Mexico City, Mexico.

1976

In August, the building owned by Trinity MCC in Riverside, CA is totally destroyed by fire. In October, King of Peace MCC in St. Petersburg, FL loses their building in a fire.

UFMCC's lay-oriented spiritual renewal program,EXCEL (Exercise in Christian Community Living) is introduced in Los Angeles.

UFMCC moves its offices from the Mother Church to the Los Angeles Gay & Lesbian Center on Highland Avenue in Hollywood.

Rev. Delolres (Dee) Jackson is the first African-American to be licensed as a clergyperson in UFMCC.

General Conference VII August 1976 Washington, DC
Theme: Proclaim Liberation In The Land
Guest Speaker at the conference, Dr. John E. Boswell,
Assistant Professor of Medieval History at Yale University.
Rev. Nancy Wilson and Rev. Charlie Arehart
are elected to the Board of Elders.

IN JANUARY 1973, REV. PERRY WAS IN DENVER, COLORADO when news that the LA church at Twenty-Second and Union had burned. Later, as he stood, deeply discouraged, in the rubble of the sanctuary, Rev. Perry thought, "The antithesis of everything Jesus ever preached created this debris," and he knew people were watching for his next move. His good friend, Willie Smith, came to him and said, "My God, Troy, the church didn't burn down. These ruins are just the closet. The church is still intact... Look at all of us who are out here in the open—we are the church! They call us faggots. They say, 'Throw another faggot on the fire!' but, we will not run. No matter what the damn fools do to us. We bend but we will not break. We are the Church and the Church will survive."

The next day, Rev. Perry held a church service on Union Street beside the blackened shell. A thousand people sat on folding chairs directly in front of a temporary altar and unanticipated hundreds stood as far as a block and a half away. They came in a time of adversity not to a wake, but to worship under the clear blue sky. They sang hymns and showed their faces to the world. Willie Smith was right—the closet had burned down!

Over the next nine years, seventeen sites where MCC congregations worshiped were targeted by arsonists. Three fires occurred in 1973 alone and the last of those was a nightmare which claimed the lives of 29 people. The site, a New Orleans bar, was torched while patrons were inside, trapped by exits blocked in such a way that they could not escape. The event propelled Rev. Troy Perry into a series of complicated interactions with the Mayor and Police of New Orleans, the Governor of Louisiana and the Archbishop of New Orleans. This was one of the first occasions when a priest refused publicly to sanction the burial of a homosexual—just one act that served as catalyst to the growth of MCC's advocacy for those who have no voice.

Rev. Elder Carol Cureton speaks
at General Conference in Denver, CO.

the Cosmopolitan HOTEL

President Jimmy Carter invites Rev. Troy Perry to attend a White House meeting. The planned discussion includes the status of Gay and Lesbian rights in the United States.

In September, Rev. Perry begins a fast on the steps of the Federal Building in Los Angeles to raise $100,000 for the fight against the Briggs Initiative, which would ban gays and lesbians from teaching in California public schools. Within 16 days, contributions from across the nation allow Rev. Perry to end his fast. The initiative is defeated and MCCs in many cities continue to fight similar initiatives through organized efforts and education.

In October, the building owned by Casa de Cristo MCC in Phoenix, AZ is firebombed.

1977

UFMCC Board of Elders approves the formation of the Committee on Lay Concerns (later renamed the Commission on Laity) and is tasked with enhancing the communication between laity and clergy.

General Conference VII August 1977 Denver, Colorado
Theme: Think On These Things
Guest Speakers include Ms. Susan Savell, United Church of Christ
Board of Homeland Ministries;
Gregory Baum, professor of Theology and Religious Studies at St. Michael's
College at the University of Toronto.
The General Conference votes to convene biennially, canceling the 1978
Conference planned for Toronto.

After the Paris Peace accords (1973) and the final, scrambling evacuation of the US embassy in Saigon (1975), the Vietnam War was at last over. But in 1977 gay Americans faced a different and very real fear. Their vocations, freedom and lives were threatened by thousands of unreasonably frightened religious folk who were provoked into near-hysteria by a handful of hate-mongering preachers, politicians and others who ignored the word love. In Miami, bumper stickers bearing the starkly written message "Kill a Queer for Christ" appeared. They were grim symbols of the climate in Dade County, and reigning over Miami's frenzy of self-righteousness and bigotry was Anita Bryant Green.

Dade County became a topic of national interest and Johnny Carson made fun of Anita's image on NBC's Tonight Show night after night. Nevertheless, Dade County voters went to the polls in record numbers on June 7th and almost 70 percent of them voted against gay people. Thousands of gay people in other cities and states took to the streets in candlelight vigils but, in truth, some paranoia had set in and with some justification. Anti-gay forces in the US were proud of their Florida success and were making new preparations to drive gays and lesbians back into the closet. A growing backlash against gays spread like wildfire and appalled gay people began to cut out pink cloth triangles, the badge the Nazi's required homosexuals to wear in the concentration camps, and stitch them to their shirts and jackets.

In 1978 the ultimate battle was waged over the Briggs Initiative in California. Political analysts believed that the initiative, written to prevent gays and lesbians from teaching in California public schools, would, if it were passed, effectively end the forward movement of gay rights in the US. Opponents of the initiative worked tirelessly to build a coalition of concerned citizens and to get the word out through celebrities. Rev. Perry launched a hunger strike to raise $100,000 for the anti-Briggs efforts and drank only water for sixteen days. In the end, the initiative was defeated by a margin of some 1.25 million votes.

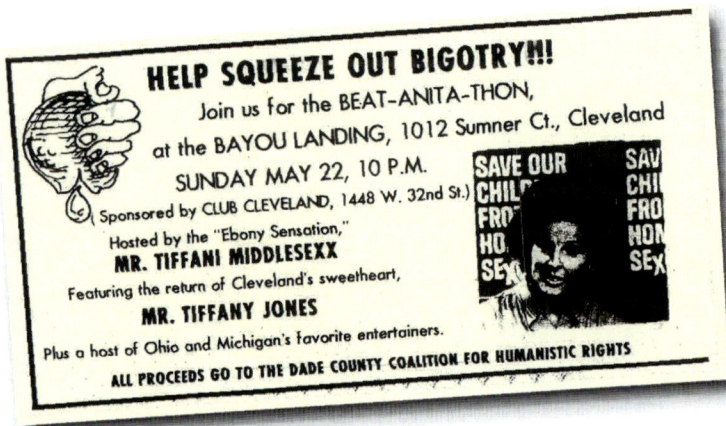

HELP SQUEEZE OUT BIGOTRY!!!
Join us for the BEAT-ANITA-THON,
at the BAYOU LANDING, 1012 Sumner Ct., Cleveland
SUNDAY MAY 22, 10 P.M.
Sponsored by CLUB CLEVELAND, 1448 W. 32nd St.)
Hosted by the "Ebony Sensation,"
MR. TIFFANI MIDDLESEXX
Featuring the return of Cleveland's sweetheart,
MR. TIFFANY JONES
Plus a host of Ohio and Michigan's favorite entertainers.
ALL PROCEEDS GO TO THE DADE COUNTY COALITION FOR HUMANISTIC RIGHTS

Rev. Jeri Ann Harvey
is called to the pastorate
of MCC-LA. She is
the first woman to fill the
position.

1978

UFMCC moves its
offices to Hollywood.

In January, the KKK
burns a cross on the lawn
of MCC of the Resurrection
in Houston, TX.

Also in 1978, San Francisco's Mayor George Moscone and City Supervisor Harvey Milk, a homosexual, were assassinated. Milk, along with comic Robin Tyler, had been an early proponent for a great march into Washington. By year's end a committee for the March was formed in Minneapolis and a national organizational structure was put into place. Marchers would demand of the leaders of the United States: (1) a National Gay and Lesbian Civil Rights Bill; (2) repeal of existing antigay laws; (3) an executive order from the President banning military, federal and federally-related discrimination on the basis of sexual orientation; (4) an end to unfair bias against homosexual parents in child custody cases; and (5) the protection of homosexual youth from discrimination.

Harvey Milk, assassinated San Francisco City Supervisor and early proponent for a great march on Washington DC for gay rights.

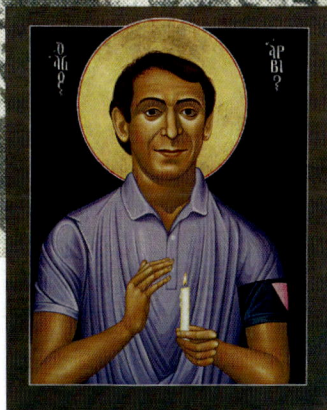

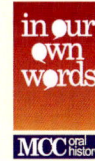

in our own words
MCC oral history

I walked in, and as I was walkin' in, there was a guy...the greeter was at the door sayin' that they'd gotten a bomb threat, and the TV crew were threatening to come, and that if I sat on one side of the church I'd definitely be on TV, but if I sat on the other side of the church I wouldn't be, and I had a choice to make if I wanted to come in the service or not that day.

And so my partner and I...chose to also sit on the side where the TV was gonna be—if we're gonna come out, just come on out—get it out of the way.

But for me, when I walked in, there was a huge sense of peace, I think, that happened within me. 'Cause growing up in the church—I'd left the church for a while because I wasn't sure where I would fit in at the church, then when I came out I was like, "well, there is no place for me in church." And so there was a big gap of about...for years I didn't do anything, no church or nothing unless I went home...it was like..."there's hope, I can find a place here."

Rev. Wanda Floyd,
Durham, North Carolina, USA

Rev. Jeri Ann Harvey, a Native American, is the first person of color to be elected to the Eldership.

300,000 participants join in the first National March on Washington for Gay and Lesbian Rights. MCC participants from across the nation make up a large number of the marchers and MCC sponsors worship services at the Lincoln Memorial.

1979

UFMCC's increasingly international composition is extended when Rev. Jean White of London, England is elected as an Elder.

General Conference IX August 1979 Los Angeles, California
Theme: For Such A Time As This
Guest speakers include Rosalind Rinker, author of *Prayer: Conversing With God*;
Virginia Mollenkott, co-author of *Is the Homosexual My Neighbor?*;
Ed Asner; Actor and activist; and
Harry Britt, San Francisco Supervisor.
Rev. Jean White and Rev. Jeri Ann Harvey are elected as Elders.

I was raised Pentecostal, my parents were Pentecostal Ministers. When I was at University, I googled the words "gay church Sydney" and MCC came up. I was coming out and I was doing ministry at my Pentecostal Church and I couldn't continue and a whole scandal happened at the Church because my parents were ministers there and I needed someplace else to go to.

I've been going to MCC for five years now. MCC is going somewhere. Because of who we are and where we are in our history now there is this passion about where we're going next.

Rev. Karl Hand,
Sydney, New South Wales, Australia

Robin Tyler and her partner Diane Olson.

OCTOBER 14 WAS SET AS THE DATE for the March and arrangements were made for affordable travel on an Amtrak train, dubbed "The Freedom Train" to run across the North American continent from San Francisco. At least 100,000 people gathered (some estimates run as high as 300,000) and though the March was smaller than hoped, it was a success in that it demonstrated to a coalition of people their ability to handle event logistics and to assemble large numbers of vocal, visible homosexuals to demonstrate for freedom.

During this time of radical defense of basic human rights in the US, the global scope of MCC was expanding. Rev. Jean White, a UK citizen, was licensed as a minister of MCC in 1978, and in 1979 she was elected to the Board of Elders. As an Elder she pastored MCC in London and was the chair and executive secretary of the World Church Extension. It was her task to educate people outside the USA that MCC was not just an American Church, but rather was a church begun in America that had a message for the entire world. Rev. Elder White said, "We must never forget that we are Christ's ambassadors to hostile lands—particularly for gay and lesbian folk."

Her thoughts paralleled those of Rev. Elder Nancy Wilson, who had first introduced the possibility of interreligious affiliation

In July MCC Tallahassee is the target of arson.

Representing UFMCC, Rev. Troy Perry testifies in Washington, DC at the first US Congressional briefing on Civil Rights for Gays and Lesbians.

Thousands of gay and lesbian Cubans flee from the port of Mariel to the United States and are held in concentration camp-style facilities. UFMCC and other groups work together to resettle these refugees.

1980

MCC members participate in "The Trek". The eight day journey from Jacksonville, FL to the state capitol in Tallahassee is called by UFMCC's Southeast District for the purpose of "witnessing to the larger community about Gay and Lesbian Spirituality" and to "witness to the Gay Community about that same Spirituality."

Rev. Don Eastman

to the General Conference of MCC. In 1981, MCC applied for membership in the National Council of Churches of Christ in the USA. The last pages of the application to the National Council, written by Adam DeBaugh, read: "In thirteen years, the UFMCC has grown considerably and often in the face of tremendous adversity and challenge from outside. Over twelve of our churches have been destroyed by arson, percentages unequaled in any other communion to our knowledge. Our clergy and lay people have been threatened, beaten and even killed. Our church buildings have been desecrated and vandalized. Our congregations have been denied places to meet for worship. Crosses have been burned on our church property; threats have been made over the telephone, in person and in print to our people. We have been attacked in the name of the Jesus we follow. And, a small minority has attacked our right to join in fellowship with our brother and sister Christians in the National Council of Churches. Why? We are criticized because we minister in a loving and caring way to a despised and rejected minority—homosexuals. It is our acceptance of homosexuality as a gift of God that arouses fear, anger and hatred. We would remind our brothers and sisters of the section of the bylaws of the NCC which requires that member communions demonstrate a spirit of cooperation and respect for the convictions of other communions. We call upon the National Council of Churches to examine our application on its merits not on false issue of our position on homosexuality."

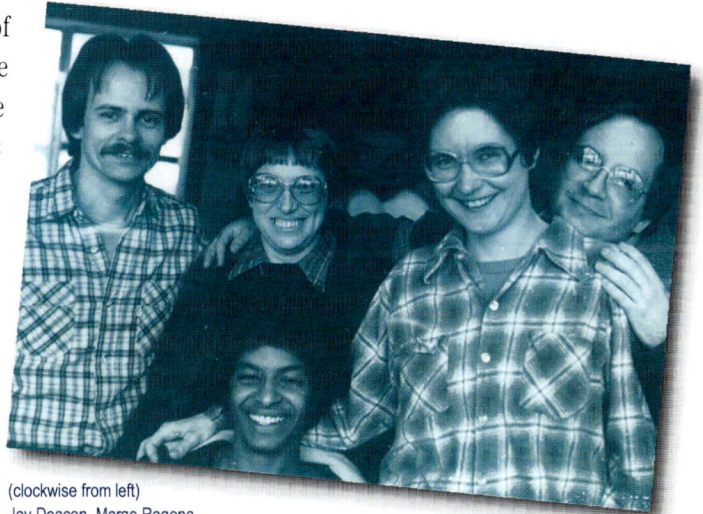

(clockwise from left)
Jay Deacon, Marge Ragona,
Val Bouchard, Keith Spare and Lucia Chappelle.

General Conference amends and approves the report of the Task Force on Inclusive Language. The report includes basic definitions and guidelines for use of inclusive language. In response to those guidelines, the Conference amends the UFMCC Statement of Faith.

Ongoing dialogue with the larger Christian community is formalized when UFMCC applies for membership in the National Council of Churches of Christ in the USA.

The first references to what will later be called AIDS begin to appear in medical journals and press reports. MCC congregations around the world mobilize in response, exhibiting leadership, compassion and courage as they learn to minister in the midst of the blossoming crisis.

1981

General Conference X August 1981 Houston, Texas
Theme: By No Other Name
Guest speakers include Joan L. Clark, Ecumenical Women's Center, Chicago;
Dr. Loretta J. Williams, Associate Professor of Sociology at the University of Missouri;
Dr. James S. Tinney, political scientist, educator, editor-publisher and black Pentecostal historian;
Rabbi Allen Bennett, Congregation Sha'ar, San Francisco.
Election of Michael Mank, UFMCC's first lay Elder and Licensure of Rev. Hong Tan, UFMCC's first Asian clergy member.
Bylaw revision which affirms "the Universal priesthood of all believers."

THE NATIONAL COUNCIL RESPONDED that such an approach would be "impertinent foolishness," and referred the application internally for a one-year study of the issues. The NCC made no decision the next year, and though all action on the application was postponed indefinitely in 1984, MCC did have a tremendous impact on the National Council of Churches. One of the bright moments in the continuing dialogue occurred when an Orthodox theologian turned to Rev. Elder Nancy Wilson and said, "I think what MCC is saying about religion not centering on sexuality is much like what Copernicus said—that the earth revolves around the sun, and not the sun around the earth." But change and enlightenment evolve slowly—we must persist.

Peggy Campolo (pictured at left) later described the persistent witness of MCC: "I believe that the MCC Church [has been] God's Nova Hutta—the ecumenical church for which Jesus prayed the night before he was crucified. The main body of the church out there is not the church for which Jesus prayed, not when it is divided and not when it shuts out those children of God who happen not to be straight. ...[MCC has] built churches that truly are ecumenical...to show the rest of the Church what it means to be in fellowship with all of the family of God. It is God's gift to you, the fellowship of those who suffer, that you have been chosen and gifted to show your brothers and sisters how well God's work in this world can be done when people are not divided by minor issues or separated because they do not see the small stuff in exactly the same way."

In September, MCC Atlanta becomes the 17th church in the fellowship to suffer fire damage.

The National Council of Churches of Christ in the USA refers UFMCC's application for membership to the NCC's Commission of Faith & Order for a year-long study of "the ecclesiological issues raised by this application."

1982

Tribulation Years

MCC's endurance, patience and faith is tested. MCC Atlanta is the 17th church to be seriously damaged or destroyed by fire. The National Council of Churches postpones indefinitely any action on MCC's membership. Rev. Virgil Scott is severely beaten and stabbed to death. MCC provides compassionate care for thousands of people with HIV/AIDS, and establishes the world-wide vigil now known as World AIDS Day.

Nova Hutta was a socialist utopian city founded by Polish communists following World War II. Its planners hoped it would provide decent housing and health services for everyone, excellent schools for all children, green spaces scattered throughout the city, a crime-free environment, and dignity-preserving care for the elderly. What Nova Hutta was intended to do is exactly what the church of Jesus Christ is to do in our world: be a single community that serves as an example of what the entire world will one day be like. We should be one people, bound together in Christian love, cultivating a social system embodying what the commonwealth will be like when it comes on earth, as it already is in heaven. To this end, during the era of growth, the General Conference of MCC voted unanimously to recommend that every member church begin working toward the use of inclusive language.

Illustrator and author, Jean Gralley chronicled the General Conference in Toronto, Ontario. During the Conference, Canada experienced a "one-hundred year heat wave."

In San Francisco, the National Council of Churches of Christ requests the opportunity to attend a typical UFMCC worship service. MCC's communion has a particularly powerful effect on NCCC members who have never before received communion together due to their inability to agree on the form of the service.

UFMCC holds its first General Conference outside the United States. The "right of all ministers, clergy and laity to celebrate and consecrate communion with equal validity" is affirmed at the Conference.

1983

General Conference XI July 1983 Toronto, Ontario, Canada
Theme: Many Gifts, One Spirit
Guest speaker is Dr. Virginia Mollenkott, author of *Women, Men and the Bible*.
A "100-year heat wave" and non-air-conditioned meeting spaces
hit the General Conference. Paramedics remain parked nearby so they can
respond quickly when called.

"Therefore, having been justified by faith, we have peace with God through our Lord Jesus Christ, through whom also we have access by faith into this grace in which we stand, and rejoice in hope of the glory of God. And not only that, but we also glory in tribulations, knowing that tribulation produces perseverance; and perseverance, character; and character, hope. Now hope does not disappoint, because the love of God has been poured out in our hearts by the Holy Spirit who was given to us."

Romans 5:1-5

In 1983, Dr. Marcus Conant of San Francisco presented the Reagan White House with a statement in which the he detailed the public health problem of AIDS in no uncertain terms. Dr. Conant was urgently focused on penetrating President Reagan's bureaucratic shield and he warned emphatically, "Western civilization has not confronted an epidemic of this magnitude in the twentieth century...emergency action is desperately needed to slow the spread of this epidemic and to prevent a calamity of incalculable magnitude." In reply, executive aides told Dr. Conant something to the effect that gay men deserved AIDS, having all but asked for the disease with their behavior—that the only necessary remedy for the "gay plague" was for homosexuals to become celibate.

During the early years of the crisis, in part because AIDS was little-understood as a danger to all people—especially those living in poverty and under religious oppression—religious opportunists seized the chance to further their own ministries of disinformation. From their pulpits, they pointed their fingers at

Rev. Elder Freda Smith with Rev. Joseph Gilbert. (at left) California capital building in Sacramento.

1984

NCC — The National Council of Churches "postpones indefinitely" any action on UFMCC's application for membership.

and attacked gay men. Although there are many accounts of those times told by and about our members and friends, a few key stories demonstrate the pivotal and catalyzing manner in which MCC engaged both the tribulation of AIDS and the world's attention.

In 1986, when thousands were dying shortly after being diagnosed, Rev. David Farrell, pastor of MCC in San Diego, organized a weekend prayer vigil for people living with AIDS and their friends and families. Although nearly a thousand priests, ministers and rabbis in that area of Southern California were invited, most of them were conspicuously absent when people of all faiths assembled to pray at the Metropolitan Community Church and Rev. David said to the gathering,

"We ask the men and women [of all churches] to lead their congregations in public prayer to create in our community a climate of compassion and care and concern for all those whose lives are affected by AIDS. We hope from what we are beginning here in San Diego, a movement is going to sweep across the United States of America and every city will hold a vigil for AIDS, uniting brothers and sisters of all faiths in prayer. When he finished speaking, attendees at the vigil sang, 'We are the world, we are the children. We stand together, forever, as servants of the Lord. We're one in our commitment in answer to the call.'"

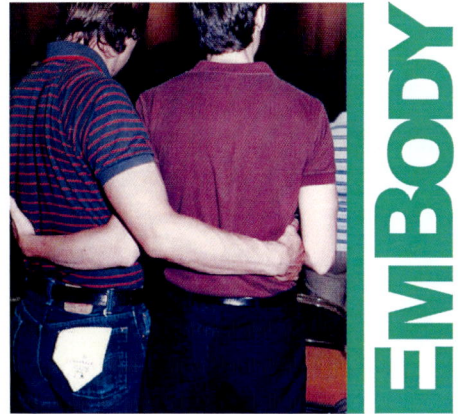

In some Islamic societies, you would never bring a sick person flowers and candies as we do in the United States. Instead you would tell them a story of patience, endurance and triumph. The images such a tale would plant in their awareness would circulate through their souls just as powerfully as a medicinal elixir would travel to the diseased cells by way of the bloodstream. The more the story is considered, the more it can empower the body's own healing mechanisms.

Richard Stone in *The Healing Art of Storytelling*

The EmBody Program of MCC's Global HIV/AIDS Ministry wants to capture your true stories about living in the time of HIV/AIDS. Log on to the MCC website and follow the link through Programs & Initiatives to Global HIV/AIDS Ministry and the EmBody Program to make your submission.

In January, MCC San Diego hosts a 50-hour AIDS Prayer Vigil for clergy and laity of all denominations.

In September, UFMCC leads 5,000 churches in a worldwide AIDS Vigil of Prayer. This event becomes the model for World AIDS Day.

1985

General Conference XII June 1985 Sacramento, California
Theme: Free To Be
A major restructuring of the Government, Structures and Systems of the Fellowship are enacted. The General Council is formed, consisting of the Board of Elders and all the District Coordinators. Translation equipment is used for the first time, making the Conference accessible to Spanish-speaking attendees.

AND, INDEED, MCC DID ANSWER THE CALL. World AIDS Day grew out of that gathering in San Diego and our prophetic witness in behalf of people living with HIV—that we are called to compassion, mercy and justice and that we are called to live gloriously, freely and with joy—has been heard around the world.

The ordeal of AIDS matured MCC in a way that perhaps nothing else could have. The women of MCC created hospices for men who were dying when no one else would care for them. The ministers of MCC, often HIV-positive themselves, conducted thousands of memorial services for those whose churches and families would not honor them. The congregations of MCC dug deeply into their resources and bought medications and food, and were active in communities all over the world in protesting the injustice of governmental and religious oppression. The Body of MCC faced the devastation with the grace, love and persistence that no one else in the world chose to offer.

Our people's response in this time of tribulation may, in many ways, represent MCC's finest hour in the first forty years of our life as a movement and a ministry.

When Rev. Steve Pieters (pictured at left), who became an influential leader in the earliest days of the epidemic, was diagnosed with AIDS and terminal cancer, he began writing extensive articles about his illness, his thoughts on numerous topics, and the art of living. He became involved with the MCC community-at-large, primarily helping people who were newly diagnosed, and was asked to appear at a private Hollywood fund-raiser to benefit AIDS research. As Steve stepped forward to speak, Shirley MacLaine, whom he had just met, took his face between her hands and said, "Just speak the truth, Reverend."

He told the assembled glitterati how, two weeks after he had been diagnosed, he had delivered an Easter sermon in which he said, "The resurrection of Jesus Christ means to me that I am free to dance, even in the face of my deadly enemy, AIDS. It means I am free to have joy, to feel God's love and have peace in my life. And so are you, my brothers and sisters, and so are you."

In February, Rev. Virgil Scott, pastor of MCC Stockton, California, is severely beaten and stabbed to death. His murder remains unsolved.

MCC is permitted to conduct religious services in low-security federal prisons.

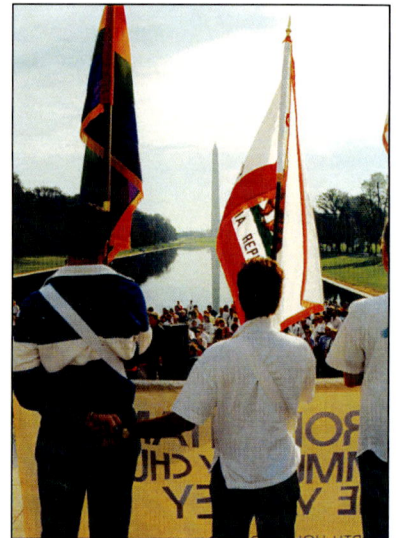

Participants in the second March on Washington with a view of the Mall from the Lincoln Memorial.

1986

Tammy Faye Bakker

In June, the United States Supreme Court rules in Bowers v. Hardwick. The Court upholds the constitutionality of a Georgia sodomy law criminalizing oral and anal sex acts occurring in private between consenting adults.

Our leadership cost us dearly but it developed us spiritually —it gave us a moist heart. According to Maria Harris in Dance of the Spirit, *First Nations' people describe spirituality as having a "moist heart," perhaps because native wisdom knows the soil of the human heart is necessarily watered with tears, and that tears keep the ground soft. From such ground new life is born.*

The Second March on Washington attracts GLBT Participants from across the USA. (at right, top) The US Supreme Court is protected during the march, And (at right) the events are chronicled in the *Los Angeles Herald.*

Gay men, lesbians and their supporters converge on Washington, DC for the second March on Washington. It is the largest gay rights demonstration ever held in the United States. Again, MCC sponsors worship services at the Lincoln Memorial.

At General Conference, a joint service is held with Dignity, a gay Roman Catholic organization. The theme is "They Will Know We Are Christians By Our Love" and peace activist, Fr. Daniel Berrigan addresses the assembly.

1987

General Conference XIII July 1987 Miami, Florida
Theme: Perfect Love Casts Out All Fear
Guest speakers include Rev. Carl Bean, Unity Fellowship of Christ Church;
Marguerite Donoghue, AIDS Action Council;
Paul Ako Kawata, Executive Director of National AIDS Network;
Lynn Lavner, entertainer.
Mr. Larry Rodriguez is elected as the second layperson to serve on the Board of Elders.

My name is Sylvanus Onyegbule Maduka.
I was born [in] Imo State, Nigeria. My spouse
is Philomena Maduka and we celebrate
our anniversary on April 1st. I grew up in the
Methodist Church [in Nigeria] and Philomena
grew up in the Catholic Church. I discovered
MCC through the Jehovah's Witness
Magazine, "Awake," in 1973 at a friend's house.
I was interested in the Church and, without
wasting time, requested from Rev. Troy Perry
to open MCC Nigeria.

Our first worship service was held on April 15,
in Kaduna State, Nigeria with 15 persons in
attendance. That first service was very
interesting and [full of joy]—there were mostly
adults and a few children. I preached the
sermon that day, "Love your neighbour as
yourself."

Rev. Sylvanus Maduka,
Okigwe, Imo State, Nigeria

God Is
Greater Than
AIDS

Metropolitan
Community Church

Then Steve surprised everyone. He began to tap dance
there as the spotlight followed him—his staccato footwork had
moments of brilliance.

Steve later met with other celebrities including Elizabeth
Taylor who eventually argued before Congress that increased
funding for AIDS could easily be taken out of the national
defense budget. He appeared on Tammy Faye Bakker's program,
"Tammy's House Party," a fundamentalist forum on the PTL
network, and told his truth. Before his segment concluded,
Tammy Faye was in tears and she said, "How sad! That we who
are Christians, who are supposed to be the salt of the earth,
who are supposed to love everyone, are so afraid of the AIDS
patient that we will not put our arms around him and tell them
that we care. I want to tell you, there are a lot of Christians here
who wouldn't be afraid to put their arms around you and tell
you that we care."

Tammy Faye paid a heavy price for that expression of
love, but she gave a priceless gift to our community. Her son,
Jay Bakker, continues that gift with his partnership in MCC's
Would Jesus Discriminate? campaign, with appearances at our
conferences and, most of all, by openly confessing God's love for all
people in every circumstance and by apologizing for the (Universal)
Church's behavior toward all sufferers, past and present.

In September 1987, at a time when vocal homosexual
Catholics were being turned out of their churches in huge numbers,
Rev. Elder Troy Perry and Rev. Elder Nancy Wilson received an

UFMCC experiences a year of growth and consolidation.
Maturing congregations set an example for each other and
for the Fellowship as a whole by making the sacrifices
necessary to purchase their own properties. A sense of
permanence and stability is created which allows for more
creative and broadly-based ministries.

1988

(At right) Jay Bakker.
(Below) Rev. Perry with Bea Bell, a guest speaker
at the Conference in St. Paul, Minnesota.

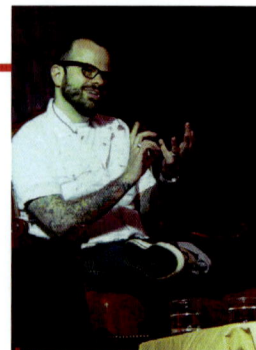

invitation to attend a mass with Pope John Paul II in Columbia, South Carolina. Because they were guests, there was little they felt they could do to address the issues involving homosexuals and AIDS directly, so they decided to witness by wearing buttons that said, "God is Greater than AIDS. Metropolitan Community Church."

The buttons and the button-wearers were noticeable, appearing as they did in a group of some four-hundred otherwise soberly-clad clergy members. Ministers approached them to read the message—some offered thanks, others rejection. The stadium held 75,000 spectators and one individual there unfurled and held a rainbow flag throughout the service. Three people stood in solidarity that day—Rev. Troy and Rev. Nancy and a lone flag bearer. No one would ever forget.

These stories—of Rev. Farrell's prayer vigil, of Rev. Pieters' tap dance, of Tammy Faye's tearful words and of Rev. Perry's and Rev. Nancy's buttons at the Pope's event, have been lived out in similar ways and thousands of times by people of MCC around the world. Each time we stand up and speak up and extend the smallest act of compassion and understanding, we change the world. This has been our blessing as a ministry—a ministry that was given to us because we could handle it in the Name of God. May we be ever-present in those moments when God creates a tsunami of spiritual awakening beneath a seemingly insignificant surface.

(Pictured above) Rev. Elder John Hose.
(At right) In 1985, Rev. David Farrell receives the John H. Hose Award during the General Conference in Calgary, Alberta, Canada.

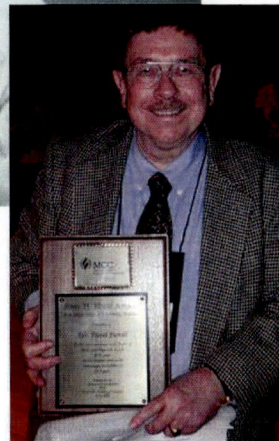

The Women's Secretariat is created in response to the continuing need to address the concerns of women.

1989

General Conference XIV July 1989 St. Paul, Minnesota
Theme: Good News For All People
The guest speaker is Beatrice Bell, death penalty opponent
and mother of one of the victims of the Atlanta Child Murder case

AS THE 1990s APPROACHED, Metropolitan Community Church congregations were still deeply engaged in supporting the needs of people living with HIV and AIDS. "Compassion fatigue" began to overwhelm many who had worked tirelessly for more than five years to provide primary care, to bury the dead and to fight both governmental and homophobic religious authorities without ceasing. In less than ten years MCC lost more than one-third of its senior male pastorate to AIDS-related death, and many of those remaining experienced burn out and could not continue to serve as pastors. Most organizations would have folded in the face of such monumental loss and devastating grief, but Rev. Troy Perry says, "You have to listen to the voice of God when you look death in the face," and MCC was in the perfect place to listen deeply when God called us again to "bring good news to the afflicted, to proclaim liberty to the captives, sight to the blind, to let the oppressed go free and to proclaim a year acceptable to God." (Luke 4:18)

In 1990, President George H.W. Bush signed the *Hate Crimes Statistics Act* into law; it was the first federal statute in US history to specifically name and recognize lesbian, gay and bisexual people. Rev. Elder Don Eastman was among the individuals invited to the White House for the signing ceremony. In 1992 in Argentina, Rev. Roberto Gonzales chained himself to the door of the Vatican Embassy to protest the homophobic pronouncements of the Archbishop of Buenos Aires.

It is said by the masters that even a little poison can cause death, and even a tiny seed can become a large tree. And as Buddha said: "Do not overlook negative actions merely because they are small: however small a spark may be, it can burn down a haystack as big as a mountain." Similarly he said, "Do not overlook tiny good actions, thinking they are of no benefit: even tiny drops of water in the end will fill a huge vessel."

Sollya Rinpoche
in *The Tibetan Book of Living and Dying*

The Elders' Task Force on Structures and Systems is created to explore and make recommendations for the next structural developments in UFMCC.

President George H. W. Bush signs the *Hate Crimes Statistics Act*, the first federal statute to recognize and name lesbian, gay and bisexual people and include them with minority groups. The law orders a detailed statistical report of crimes motivated by racial, ethnic, religious or anti-gay bias. Rev. Elder Don Eastman (pictured below at left, with Rev. Jim Sandmire) is among those invited to the White House for the signing ceremony.

1990

Human Rights Years

President George H. W. Bush signs the *Hate Crime Statistics Act*. Rev. Elder Don Eastman is at the White House for the signing ceremony. Women comprise 43% of MCC 305 clergy. Rev. Roberto Gonzales chains himself to the Vatican Embassy in Buenos Aires. Troy Perry unites 2000 gay couples at the National March in Washington DC.

In January 1994, MCC's "Mother Church" in Los Angeles was destroyed in a devastating earthquake—seventy-nine other churches of various denominations were destroyed or badly damaged as well. A week after the earthquake, Larry Stammer of the LA Times asked the question, "Is Quake a Sign of God's Wrath?" and a number of voices claimed that Southern California—perceived by some as a center of lewd and licentious lifestyles—was a special target of God's wrath. Once again, some of our own members grew afraid and advocated a retreat to the closet. Some churches asked Rev. Perry to not preach because he was such a public figure and too "out."

Again faced with a decision about MCC's true calling in the world, Rev. Troy led with these words: "I believe with all of my heart that it is not enough ... for people of faith to simply

A non-binding resolution calling for workshops "reflecting the theological and spiritual diversity of UFMCC" is issued to address healthy tensions occuring around theological and liturgical issues.

The denomination moves toward sex/gender equality. The percentage of women clergy grows steadily, and now women comprise 43% of UFMCC's 305 clergy.

1991

For the first time, programming for children is included at the General Conference. At the other end of the age-spectrum, the Board of Pensions is established to administer a retirement plan for UFMCC clergy in the United States.

General Conference XV July 1991 Phoenix, Arizona
Theme: I Have Opened A Door
Guest speakers include Urvashi Vaid, Executive Director NLGTF;
Daniel Maguire, Professor of Moral Theology at Marquette University, Milwaukee;
Alexandra M. Levine, Professor of Medicine, UCLA
Rev. Willem (Bill) Hein, now Rev. Wilhelmina Hein, is the
first transgendered person elected to the Board of Elders.

pray for something. As much as I believe in the power of prayer, I also believe we must put legs on our prayers ... Our actions create the open doors through which God works. And sometimes, 'putting feet to our prayers' means we are required to speak up and to speak out.

I learned a long time ago that even well-meaning people in government could not understand the importance of GLBT rights unless someone talked to them and raised their consciousness of the issues ... I am amazed by how much has changed in our world over the past few decades—all because so many people have refused to deny our own existence in exchange for peace and quiet. If you are serious about living a liberated life, one of the most important things you can do is be yourself and to live your life with openness and authenticity. All external change in our world begins first with internal change and internal acceptance. And we will never end the external oppression in our world until we first end our internal oppression."

Los Angeles Times

MONDAY, APRIL 26, 1993

Huge March Seeks Gay Rights

Exit Polls Point to Win for Yeltsin

One million gays, lesbians, friends and family gather and march in the streets of Washington D.C. The Los Angeles Times stated: "...they paraded slowly past the White House toward the Capitol waving signs, singing songs, shouting slogans and wearing T-shirts declaring their pride."

The UFMCC 1992 People of Color Conference registers 131 attendees and is the largest and most spirited event of its type to date.

In New Zealand, UFMCC members work with other lesbian/gay organizations to include sexual orientation in a national anti-discrimination act to be considered by Parliament in 1993.

1992

In Argentina, Rev. Roberto Gonzalez is among a group who chain themselves to the door of the Vatican Embassy to protest the homophobic pronouncements of the Archbishop of Buenos Aires.

The first UFMCC District Conference to be held in a country where English is not the primary language takes place in Hamburg, Germany. EXCEL International achieves its goal of having an EXCEL weekend in every UFMCC District.

This prophetic witness propelled MCC to the realization that we had already entered an era of intense involvement in human rights.

In 1997, Rev. Perry participated in the White House Conference on Hate Crimes and in that same year, was honored by President Clinton for his contributions to society. Rev. Perry also went to South Africa where he met with Nobel Peace Prize winner, Archbishop Desmond Tutu. When Matthew Shepard was murdered in 1998, Rev. Perry and Rev. Jesse Jackson responded by holding a joint rally in Los Angeles—an event which became a public statement against hate crimes and marked the start of a national movement. The World Council of Churches, meeting in Zimbabwe, invited MCC to present a public worship service in which many attendees experienced the "open table" for the first time.

The issue of same-sex marriage became headline news during this time. Although skeptics told Rev. Perry he was beating his head against an immovable wall, many people in our communities around the world fought long and hard for marriage rights. Holland and Belgium were the first countries to extend full marriage rights to same-sex couples and others have since followed. Still others have adopted legal protections that afford up to 90% or greater equivalency to traditional marriage rights, and in May of 2008, the California Supreme Court struck down a ban on same-sex marriage in Rev. Troy's home state.

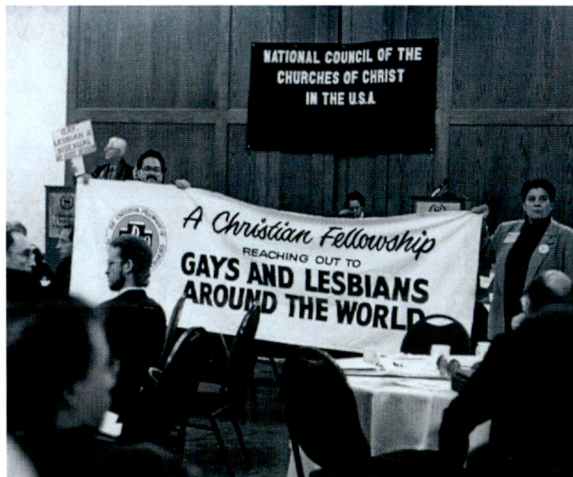

MCC representatives lead a protest at a National Council of Churches General Board meeting in November of 1992.

To celebrate their love and to demonstrate for lesbian/gay couples' rights, 2000 gay couples are united by Rev. Troy Perry at "The Wedding," one of the events sponsored by UFMCC during the National March on Washington. One million participants converge on Washington, and again, UFMCC hosts worship at the Lincoln Memorial.

Rev. Hong Tan is the first Asian, and Rev. Darlene Garner is the first African-American to be elected as Elders in the fellowship.

The General Board of the National Council of Churches votes to "take no action" on UFMCC's request for observer status. Declaring it "easier to get into heaven than the NCCC!" Rev. Elder Nancy Wilson reports that UFMCC will continue to have a presence at all NCCC General Board meetings, but will not pursue further dialogue with the organization.

1993

General Conference XVI July 1993 Phoenix, Arizona
Theme: For All The Nations
Guest speakers include Dr. Alexandra Levine, M.D., Professor of Medicine;
Father John McNeill, adjunct Professor and author of *The Church And The Homosexual*;
Dr. Mel White, former ghostwriter for many figures of the religious right;
Marie Fortune, author of *Is Nothing Sacred?*...;
Rebecca Sevilla, president of Movimiento Homosexual de Lima (Peru);
Suzanne Haynes, National Cancer Institute in Bethesda, MD;
David Mixner, campaign manager, fund raiser and political strategist

Re-Newal Years

The General Council votes to purchase the West Hollywood property. The first MCC website goes on-line. The World Council of Churches invites MCC to provide public worship. Restructuring begins and is completed, and marriage rights for all are offered in the state of California.

...There were probably 5 women in the room and maybe 80 men or something...among the communion servers, one was a woman. And so they had that awareness already... women in leadership. And so they invited everyone to come to communion if you know Christ or are seeking Christ.

I didn't know if I was, but I wanted to go to communion, so I did. And I went to the woman, who was Betty Nelson in the Portland MCC, and she gave me, you know, the communion and as she prayed over me she said, "Mother-Father-God..." and began to pray.

And I thought, "I can't believe I'm hearing the word 'mother' in a Christian church," and that was 1977 so this is like really early. But she said she felt moved by the Spirit to say that, and that's really why I stayed and why I came back.

Rev. Dr. Frodo Okulam,
Portland, Oregon, USA

MCC has also confronted the US government's policy of "Don't Ask, Don't Tell." Rev. Perry testified before the Congress and spoke one-on-one with the President about it. In 2002, the Federal Government approved MCC's request to be able to supply chaplains to the United States Veterans Administration, a historic step for government programs that had been openly hostile to the LGBT community.

By the year 2000, Metropolitan Community Church was operating throughout the world either as a ministry or a human rights movement, but the intense work strained the system almost to the point of breaking both financially and emotionally. Rev. Perry's announcement that he would step down at age sixty-five gave MCC a period of several years to plan the major organizational transition necessitated by the retirement of such a charismatic leader. MCC engaged some of the most highly qualified consultants for church transition in the world to help assess what would be required to handle the change, and in addition, a 55-member team (see page 59) was named to help lead the process of transformation and renewal. The document "Moving Forward in Faith" was published and more than 5000 MCC congregants participated in surveys and forums related to the ultimate restructuring recommendations for MCC operations worldwide.

With renovations underway, the facilities of MCC Los Angeles are destroyed by the devastating Northridge earthquake. A new property is located, and in 1995, UFMCC's General Council votes unanimously to authorize negotiating the purchase of this modern building complex on Santa Monica Blvd. in West Hollywood, California. The ambitious joint-project between UFMCC and MCC-LA will provide a future home for both entities.

1994

Rev. Elder Troy Perry with members of Sister Spirit MCC in Portland, Oregon.

Over the past [30-plus] years, the UFMCC has [thrice] adopted major changes to its structures and systems…Two key issues were raised…yet never adequately addressed. One is that there is a disparity between districts…The other…was Global Outreach…The current structure mitigates against churches located outside of districts having full access to the resources, support, and training for ministry that are available to district churches. [Nor does it] allow churches in Global Outreach to have full access to the UFMCC governance systems.

Two additional issues have also emerged…the role, structure, and nominating process for the Board of Elders…[and] the need to assure effective stewardship and a reasonable level of local church contribution to support denominational ministry. The Board of Elders raised all four of the issues during General Conference in 1999…We are at the threshold of transfer of leadership to the next generation…we must determine what structures will best serve our future.

Excerpted from *Moving Forward in Faith*

"No one puts new wine into old wineskins; otherwise the wine will burst the skins and it will be spilled out, and the skins will be destroyed. But new wine must be put into fresh wineskins."

Luke 5: 37–38

At General Conference, Rev. Perry shares his "Vision…For the Next Generation." The Conference enthusiastically approves the proposal for a joint Capital Campaign venture between UFMCC and MCC-LA to raise the $3.8 million needed to purchase the new property (pictured at right).

Our Tribe: Queer Folks, God, Jesus and The Bible by Rev. Nancy Wilson is published.

1995

General Conference XVII July 1995 Atlanta, Georgia
Theme: All Things Are Possible
Guest speakers include Chandler Burr, author of *In Search of the Gay Gene*;
Dr. Randall Bailey, Associate Professor of Old Testament, Hebrew,
Biblical Studies and Languages at the Interdenominational Theological Center in Atlanta;
Eric Rofes, author of *Reviving the Tribe*;
Dr. Elizabeth Stuart, Senior Lecturer in Theology at the University of Glamorgan, Wales, UK

The wonderful thing about MCC is that not only is the leadership inspirational, but it taught me that I would find inspiration in God talking to me through the most unlikely people —people who would never have a title or a position. That's constantly happening to me in MCC, so I know God is really here.

I've been a member of maybe eight MCC's in my long career and I love this Church so much. My pastor at MCC NoVa, Rev. Kharma Amos, is a fabulous leader because she steps back and in very skillful ways draws out people to do what needs to be done. I really love my Church community there very, very much. MCC is alive and well in that little Church. And it's cutting edge; I always like to be there.

Jean Gralley,
Potomac Falls, Virginia, USA

Perhaps the largest single factor in the deliberations was the need to address the two-fold, global character of MCC as a human rights movement as well as a church. Organizationally, Global Outreach was not achieving its goals in terms of planting financially viable churches and many people outside the USA did not feel included in the voice of MCC. In addition, the existing structure comprising Districts, the Board of Elders and the General Council was not able to sustain an equitable level of resourcing for churches inside and outside the United States. A sweepingly bold change was proposed to and adopted by the General Conference: Districts were eliminated in favor of global Regions that, by design, did not follow typical geographic lines and would force the organization to deal with everyone at the table in terms of diversity and experience. As a result, some combinations of cities, states and nations initially felt very awkward and, in fact, raised some very serious questions about our real commitment to "The Other" in our own midst.

Life itself is hazardous. There are sharp rocks everywhere. What changes from years of practice is coming to know something you didn't know before: that there are no sharp rocks—the road is covered with diamonds.

Charlotte Joko Beck in *Nothing Special*

On May 1, the UFMCC establishes a presence in cyberspace with its first website: www.ufmcc.com.

In June, UFMCC and MCC-LA complete Phase One of the Capital Campaign and in August a Celebration of Thanksgiving and Blessing is held on the new property. The beautiful facilities become the new home for UFMCC offices and the "Mother Church." Phase Two of the Capital Campaign gets underway to raise funds required to complete the redesign of the West Hollywood property.

1996

MCC Los Angeles continues a series of fund raising efforts in the Southern California area. Rev. Elder Perry's Capital Campaign tour of UFMCC congregations, "Vision... For the Next Generation,"visits 137 MCC congregations in the USA, Canada, the UK and France, and raises over $1,400,000 (US) in cash and pledges.

Rev. June Norris attends the General Conference of Metropolitan Community Churches in Sydney, Australia.

Triple our numbers, urges church leader

Holy homos!

"God didn't create you so he could sit around and have someone to hate."
— Rev Troy Perry

A unique mix of queer politics, camp humour and baptist-style preaching hit Sydney this week, with over 1,000 delegates and partners from the Universal Fellowship of Metropolitan Community Churches (UFMCC) arriving for the church's 18th general conference.

Established in California in the late 1960s to minister to the gay and lesbian community, UFMCC now claims over 46,000 members worldwide, and congregations in 19 countries.

"God didn't create you so he could sit around and have someone to hate," UFMCC founder Rev Troy Perry told an enthusiastic crowd of gays, lesbians, transs, bisexuals "and out friends in the heterosexual community" at the church's opening rally on Sunday at the Sydney Town Hall.

The predominantly American audience gave a standing ovation when told about the Uniting Church's Dorothy McRae-McMahon and others who came out as lesbian or gay during last week's Uniting Church general meeting.

Heather Horntvedt, from Parents and Friends of Lesbians and Gays (PFLAG), was also given an enthusiastic round of applause when she received the UFMCC's human rights award.

"This is a wonderful celebration of who we are ... we're showing our country and the world that sexuality and spirituality can be combined," Perry said.

The five day general conference at Darling Harbour ends tomorrow.

Topics on the agenda include Is AIDS a Dead Issue?; Guerilla Marketing Strategies: How to Publicize Your Church, Gain Media Attention, and Reach the Unchurched; Gay and Lesbian Parenting; and Who's "Gloria"? Exploring the Need for Reality-Based Christian Education in

MCC Chris Puplick, president of the NSW Anti-Discrimination Board, addresses a plenary session today, entitled Compassion as Public Policy.

At the general conference on Monday, the Rev Perry urged Australian delegates to triple the total number of Metropolitan Community Churches in Australia in the coming years.

Perry said the UFMCC was one of the fastest growing Christian denominations in the world, and he encouraged delegates to use technologies such *Continued Page 3 ▶*

UFMCC's rally at Sydney Town Hall ... "showing the world that sexuality and spirituality can be combined." Photo: Chris Pavlich

In November, Rev. Perry participates in the White House Conference on Hate Crimes. The day includes a breakfast meeting with President Clinton, Staff and civil rights leaders; a number of working sessions; and an evening reception with members of the President's Cabinet.

In November, Rev. Perry joins 120 religious leaders from the USA for a breakfast meeting with President Clinton. The President recognizes the leaders' contributions to society.

In December, Rev. Perry visits UFMCC congregations in South Africa and meets with Nobel Peace Prize winner, Archbishop Desmond Tutu, in Johannesburg.

1997

General Conference XVIII July 1997 Sydney, NSW, Australia
Theme: You Are The Light Of The World
Guest speakers include Dr. Chung Hyun Kyung, Professor of Ecumenics at Union Theological Seminary;
Chris Puplick, President of the Anti-Discrimination Board of New South Wales, Chair of the Australian National Council of AIDS and Related Diseases.
Limited access to the General Conference is offered for the first time over the internet.
Instant news, some live programming, reports and photos are provided.
Mr. Clark Frierson is elected to the Board of Elders.

According to Jim Wallis in *Who Speaks for God*, Dr. Beatrice Bruteau ask[ed] the right question [of MCC at this turning point in our history]: "'How big is your we?' Can we expand our vision of community beyond our own skin, family, race, tribe, culture, country, and species? Spiritual life is more than what we believe; it also includes how we relate. Who is included in the *WE* and who is not? That is both a spiritual and political question. How we answer it will likely determine our future."

Rev. Elder Hong Tan, Rev. Elder Don Eastman, Rev. Elder Nancy Wilson and other clergy participate at General Conference in Los Angeles, California. (at right) Rev. Elder Darlene Garner, Rev. Elder Don Eastman and Rev. Elder Hong Tan take part in the dedication ceremonies for the West Hollywood offices and MCC-LA building.

Rev. Troy Perry and Rev. Jesse Jackson hold a joint rally and press conference in Los Angeles in response to the murder of Matthew Shepard. The event becomes more than a public statement against hate crime— it marks the start of a national movement.

UFMCC begins a series of monthly cybercasts. The thirty-minute audio programs feature music, UFMCC musicians and messages from Rev. Elder Troy Perry.

The MCC Kids' Page goes online. The site is an outgrowth of the Children's Ministry program of MCC Charlotte.

1998

The World Council of Churches, meeting in Zimbabwe, invites UFMCC to present a public worship service for the Body. Rev. Elder Hong Tan preaches a memorable, stirring sermon, and MCC Los Angeles holds a simultaneous service as a show of support.

Rev. Dr. Candace Shultis and Col. Grethe Cammermeyer (Ret.) at General Conference 2007 in Scottsdale, AZ.

From 1999 to 2008, MCC has been engaged in a questioning of ourselves that has compelled us to challenge every policy and every practice, every tradition and every "given" in our organization. In addition, we have struggled to meet a myriad of financial demands as our reputation for tearing down walls and building up hope has grown in the wake of 9-11, Hurricane Katrina and other storms and disasters that seriously affected many of our churches.

The cumulative effect of these devastating events, in combination with the denomination's major structural shift, propelled us to a point that experts in organizational change term the "break down or break through" stage. In 2005-2006, when the last phase of the restructuring plan was implemented, Rev. Elder Troy Perry retired, Rev. Elder Nancy Wilson was elected as the Moderator of MCC and an Executive Director was hired for global operations. At that time, MCC's only significant financial asset was property in West Hollywood,

in our own words

MCC oral history

In 1984 I heard there was a gay Church, which I just thought…might be entertaining, but no way could it actually be a Church. Then I found out there was one three blocks from my home…and I went. And it WAS Church.

They were singing my favorite hymns, reading my favorite scriptures and having an actual sermon about my life, and I could go take Communion with my family. I cried through the entire service; I thought, "My God, there are other people like me!"

Not long after that…I drove up to West Hollywood. Halfway into the service, Troy said "…I want you to come up and sing your song for us."

I said, "No,…don't do that stuff anymore." But…I got up and sang. And he came up after the service and said, "I want you to write for our General Conference…"

I said, "I don't write songs anymore." He said, "Marsha, how do you know it wasn't for such a time as this that you came into the Communion of God." So, I started writing "Free To Be" for the next General Conference.

Marsha Stevens-Pino,
Tiera Verde, Florida, USA

UNCOMMON HOPE

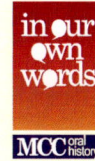

In April, UFMCC announces the inauguration of the "IntraNet de FUICM en Español"—a website with UFMCC materials presented in the Spanish language.

Rev. Robert Griffin continues to serve MCC's HIV/AIDS Ministry with excellence. He "holds the space" for an era of movement and ministry while the UFMCC waits for a flame and passion to be rekindled.

Both the President and President-Elect of the United Church of Christ attend MCC's General Conference as ecumenical guests and address the assembly. MCC announces the beginnings of bilateral discussions with the UCC about ministry and partnership.

1999

On July 11, the City of West Hollywood temporarily closes Santa Monica Blvd. and UFMCC, MCCLA, friends and family celebrate and dedicate the new UFMCC World Center and the MCC "Mother Church."

General Conference IXX July 1999 Los Angeles, California
Theme: The Joy Of God Is Our Strength
Guest speakers include Rev. Dr. Jimmy Allen, past President of the Southern Baptist Convention, author of *Burden of A Secret*;
Rev. Yvette Flunder, Senior Pastor of the City of Refuge Community Church in San Francisco;
Dr. R. Stephen Warner, professor of sociology at the University of Illinois at Chicago;
Felicia Park-Rogers, COLAGE (Children of Lesbians And Gays Everywhere);
Rev. Dr. Nori Rost is elected to the Board of Elders.

I was part of a gay/lesbian open church group in Copenhagen and we got in contact with…MCC in London, where the Rev. Elder Jean White was the Pastor. So I visited her church in 1980, and then there was a General Conference in 1981, which I went to —it was the Conference of inclusive language…And because of that Conference and…MCC Los Angeles and DeColores MCC, which was a women's community MCC …where there were feminists; I thought, "I want this Church, this is the place for me."

…I think the combination of a very deep spirituality and social justice, those two things actually go together. You cannot have the action without the spirituality and the depth of that in your faith, and you cannot have your faith and spirituality without acting and doing justice.

…One of the things I love about General Conference is when you come from a very small congregation that the feeling of how big this is, meeting so many different people and realizing how big this really is.

Rev. Mia Anderson,
Copenhagen, Denmark

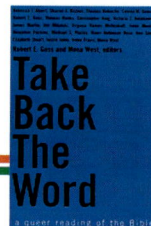

our balance sheet was "upside down," (liabilities exceeded assets) and our cash flow was at serious risk. The Board of Administration, first appointed in 2003, made the timely, courageous and controversial decision to sell the property in West Hollywood, pay off a high-interest debt and establish an endowment of $2,000,000 for MCC's next generation. Furthermore, they adopted a strategic plan which encompassed five core initiatives intended to help align MCC worldwide.

The good news is that we broke through, not down and we are moving on. Since the restructuring began, name-recognition of MCC has grown 100-fold worldwide. In Eastern Europe, we are now commonly known as the *Human Rights Church*. Rev. Elder Diane Fisher, Florin Buhuceanu and team have confronted religious orthodoxy and homophobia in such

Metropolitan Community Churches participates in the Milennium March on Washington DC.

The struggle for gay rights records two victories and a loss: Vermont becomes the first US state to legally recognize civil unions between gay or lesbian couples; the UK ban on homosexuals serving in the armed forces is abolished; and the US Supreme Court rules that the Boy Scouts of America has the right to ban gays from its ranks.

April—The Millennium March on Washington takes place. Festivities began on Saturday morning with Rev. Elder Perry conducting a mass "wedding" for same-sex couples at the Lincoln Memorial.

Take Back The Word— A Queer Reading of The Bible, edited by Rev. Robert Goss and Rev. Mona West, is published.

Take Back The Word

a queer reading of the Bible

2000

Growing spiritually can be like a roller coaster ride. Take comfort in the knowledge that the way down is only preparation for the way up.

Rebbe Nachman of Breslov in *The Empty Chair*

compelling ways that young people in that area of the world are empowered to build their own spiritual communities and are speaking up and speaking out for themselves.

In Jamaica, Rev. Robert Griffin and Sunshine Cathedral, along with MCC's Global Justice Team led by Rev. Pat Bumgardner, have helped establish and sustain a church in what is arguably the most homophobic nation in the world. Our leaders continue in dialogue with the highest offices in Jamaica regarding justice and safety for LGBT people there. We have supported the opening of the first church in Malaysia. In Latin America, we have convened the first LGBT leadership conference for faith leaders. In Africa, we have provided shelter and advocacy for 300 children who have lost their parents to HIV/AIDS. We have also supported the

Rev. Judy Dahl (center) ordains Rev. (Elder) Armando Sanchez (left) and Mario Gutierrez (right) in Nicaragua. (pictured at right) Carlos Chavez in Nicaragua.

Rev. Dr. Brent Hawkes performs a double wedding for two same-sex couples in Toronto, Ontario. Although city clerks would not issue marriage licenses, Hawkes conducted a legal marriage by employing the alternative allowed in Ontario law for regular church attendees to publish official banns for three consecutive weeks.

The need for MCC's presence in Eastern Europe is underscored when a mob of football hooligans, clerics, ultranationalist youth and far right skinheads storm the first Pride march in Belgrade (then Yugoslavia, now Serbia) attacking and seriously injuring several participants and preventing the event from taking place.

MCC's Office of Ecumenical and Interfaith ministry is eliminated due to financial struggles as well as the beginnings of the denomination's reorganization. MCC's ongoing dialogue with UCC is suspended pending the completion of the former's reorganization.

2001

General Conference XX July 2001 Toronto, Ontario, Canada
Theme: Moving Forward In Faith
Guest speakers include James Noel, Assistant Professor of American Religion at the San Francisco Theological Seminary;
Donna Red Wing, Director of Outgiving Project, Gill Foundation;
Thomas Bandy, Vice-president and senior partner in the church growth consulting firm Easum, Bandy & Associates;
Rev. Dr. Mel White, former ghostwriter for the religious right and author of *Strangers At The Gate*.
Mr. Mel Johnson is elected to the Board of Elders.

(at right) Moderator Rev. Elder Nancy Wilson;
(at far right) Rev. Elder Nancy Wilson,
Scott Long of Human Rights Watch and
Rev. Elder Diane Fisher at the Human Rights
Breakfast, General Conference 2007

(above, from left to right) Rev. Elder Nancy Wilson, Bishop Yvette A. Flunder and her partner, Shirley,
Rev. Lynice Pinkard and Nichole at the Founder's 500 Reception, General Conference 2007.
Rev. Neil Thomas, of MCC-LA, serves as Board Chair for California Faith For Equality, an organization
that seeks to educate religious communities on the importance of marriage equality for LGBT couples.
Rev. Robert Griffin.

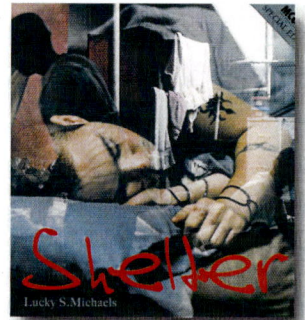

Shelter (above) began In 2003 when
Rev. Pat Bumgardner (pictured at left)
of MCC New York invited
Lucky Michaels to help open Sylvia's
Place, the first emergency shelter
for LGBTQ youth and young adults.
The Marsha P. Johnson Center,
a 24-hour drop-in facility, opened
in 2007.

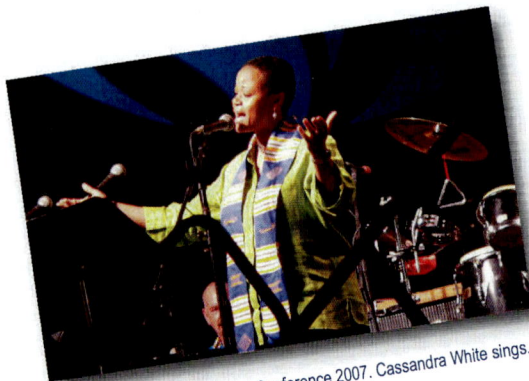

Praise and worship at General Conference 2007. Cassandra White sings.

Civil union is passed
in Buenos Aires,
making it the first Latin-
American city to
legalize same-sex
unions.

Rapid HIV testing is
approved in the
US, eliminating the
current week-long
waiting periods for
test results.

2002

(left to right) Bishop Carlton Pearson, Jay Bakker and Rev. Elder Troy Perry at General Conference 2007.

continued development of an MCC congregation in Nigeria while taking a significant role in the confrontation of that country's deadly laws. In 2008 our newly mobile REVM program made it possible for three African clergy candidates to complete the work required for them to lead churches in their respective countries.

We launched a renewal of our commitment to ministry for HIV/AIDS when most organizations were retreating, again taking the lead in an area where we have been called since the beginning of the epidemic. More than 54 churches have equipped themselves for work with and ministry to people struggling with crystal meth. We have supported the progress of more than 40 new clergy members who are highly trained and well-prepared to lead the next generation of spiritual activists. In the last three years, we have created more resources for local churches than ever before in our history: the highly effective *Creating a Life that Matters* curriculum, the interim and transitional ministry programs, the *Faith that Fits* curriculum for youth, new publications on *Homosexuality and the Bible*, transgender resources and

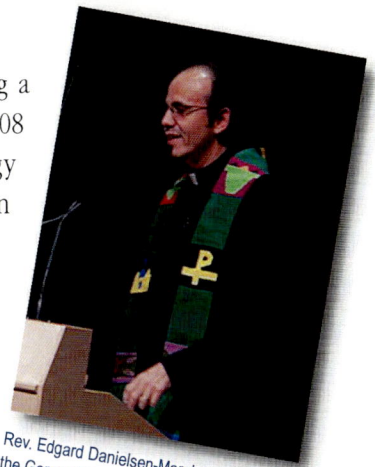

Rev. Edgard Danielsen-Morales addresses the General Conference.

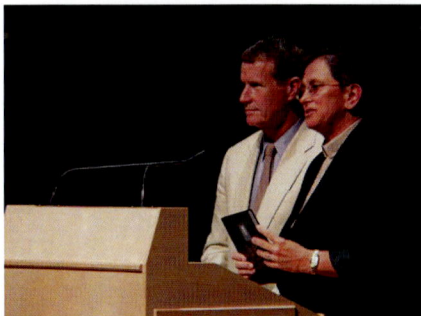

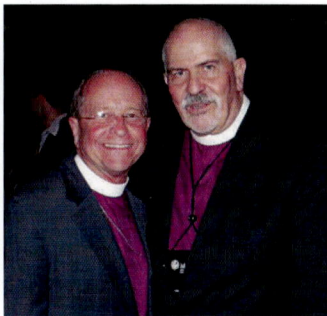

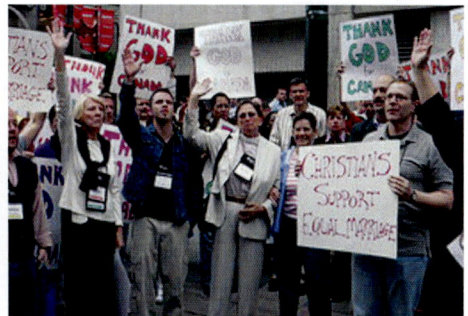

(from left to right) At General Conference, Chris Glaser and Moderator Rev. Elder Nancy Wilson; The Right Reverend V. Gene Robinson and Rev. Elder Troy Perry. MCC participates in a street rally celebrating marriage equality in Calgary, Alberta, Canada, 2005.

The Ontario Court of Appeal affirms that the marriages performed by Rev. Dr. Brent Hawkes in 2001 were legal and strikes down all barriers against same-sex marriage in the province. With this ruling, Canada becomes the first country in the Americas to honor legal same-sex marriage.

MCC's work in Eastern Europe, where human rights efforts are virtually indistinguishable from ecumenical and interfaith work, officially begins as Rev. Elder Diane Fisher assumes responsibility for the Ecumenical portfolio.

MCC holds a recommitment ceremony for persons living with HIV/AIDS and 500 march in the streets wearing t-shirts emblazoned "HIV +"

MCC members join in a street rally for marriage equality in Calgary, Alberta.

2003

General Conference XXI July 2003 Dallas, Texas
Theme: Let Your Light Shine
Guest speakers include Richard Elovich, nationally recognized trainer and program evaluation consultant in substance use and HIV;
Rev. Barbara J. Essex, Minister and Coordinator of Community Life at Pacific School of Religion in Berkeley, CA;
Barbara Gittings, gay rights activist and founder of the New York City chapter of the Daughters of Bilitis;
Theodore Jennings, Consultant to the United Methodist Church on issues related to commitment to the poor;
Speed Leas, Senior Consultant for the Alban Institute;
Ken Stone, Lambda Literary Award Winner; Esera Tuaolo, former NFL football player;
Daniel Wolfe, Community Scholar at the Columbia University School of Public Health.
Jason and deMarco (pictured at left) perform.

the *Would Jesus Discriminate?* Campaign. Our websites, On-Line Resources and our main MCCChurch.org site, serve more than 1 million people annually. We now have MCC leaders on the Board of Trustees at Pacific School of Religion, Chicago Theological Seminary and Lancaster Theological Seminary as well as a similar pending appointment at Episcopal Divinity School.

In February 2007, more than 20 MCC clergy participated in the Clergy Call for Justice and Equality in Washington, DC. The Human Rights Campaign is partnering with us for the *Would Jesus Discriminate?* Campaign and, at the time of this publication, will be in Fargo, North Dakota and Brainerd, Rochester and Minneapolis, Minnesota. During the same time, we will be leading institutes on senior housing for SAGE in New York. We recently partnered with the Institute for Welcoming Resources for the September 2008 *Many Stories, One Voice* Conference in New Orleans, and 20 of our young adults helped lead workshops there. We are actively working with SoulForce-Q throughout the United States and are represented by one

Barry Hundley leads worship at the MCC General Conference in Calgary, Alberta, Canada.

Rev. Karla Fleshman.

The global fight for civil rights/marriage rights continues to record both wins and losses. The first attempt to place an amendment to the US constitution banning marriage is defeated; Portugal's constitution is amended to protect people from discrimination on the basis of sexual orientation; civil union is realized in Brazil; Australia bans same-sex marriage, and New Zealand passes a civil union bill.

2004

In the wake of the Presidential election, GLBT civil rights groups in the US begin to explore and consider the importance of seeking input from religious groups. MCC's partnership with HRC, NGLTF, the National Black Coalition and the Marriage Coalition take on new importance.

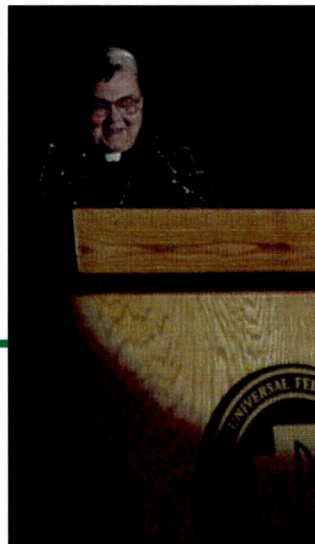
Rev. Elder Jeri Ann Harvey.

(above) Rev. Elder Nancy Wilson receives the blessing of MCC youth at the General Conference in Calgary. During her Installation Service in the National Cathedral in Washington, DC, (at left) Rev. Elder Nancy Wilson blesses the elements during Holy Communion, and (below) is received enthusiastically by the Board of Elders and congregants.

The structural transition begun in 1993 is completed. Rev. Dr. Cindi Love is appointed the first Executive Director of Metropolitan Community Churches. The global redistribution of all teams and offices begins with the acquisition of offices for the Moderator in Sarasota, Florida. "Points of presence" are established where a majority of MCC members reside—Texas, Florida and California—as well as where ministry opportunities are emerging—Latin America and Eastern Europe.

Many same-sex couples choose to be legally married while they are attending UFMCC's General Conference in Canada.

Rev. Elder Nancy Wilson is installed as UFMCC's second Moderator. The installation takes place at the National Cathedral in Washington, DC.

2005

General Conference XXII July 2005   Calgary, Alberta, Canada
Theme: A Future And A Hope
Guest speakers include Rt. Rev. V. Gene Robinson, Ninth Bishop of New Hampshire, Episcopal Church;
Amber Hollibaugh, Senior Strategist, National Gay & Lesbian Task Force;
Rt. Rev. Steven Charleston, President & Dean, Episcopal Divinity School;
Jonathan Dimmock, Founder, Art to the Nations;
Rev. Robert Chase, Executive Director Office of Communication, UCC;
Kerry Lobel, Founder & Principal, The Change Group;
Dave Nimmons, Founder, Manifest Love

People of African Descent (PAD) Conference pre-worship in St. Louis, MO.

Toronto, Canada Pride!

MCC in Sao Paulo, Brazil.

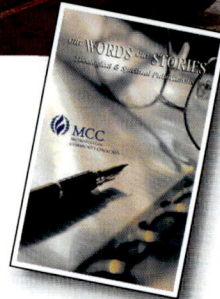
Our Words Our Stories, Theological & Spiritual Publications is compiled by Rev. Robert Goss and released in 2007.

In May, MCC partners with Faith in America and Jesus MCC in Indianapolis, Indiana USA to launch the Would Jesus Discriminate? Campaign.

MCC's Executive Director, Rev. Dr. Cindi Love, is appointed to the Faith and Religion Council for the Human Rights Campaign.

Moderator Rev. Elder Nancy Wilson is appointed to the Bishops' and Elders' Council for the National Gay and Lesbian Task Force Institute for Welcoming Resources.

2006

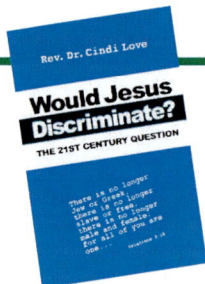

HBO releases All Aboard, Rosie O'Donnell's documentary featuring 500 families headed by non-heterosexual parents. The film highlights MCC's role in providing pastoral support to the families. Also, The Queer Bible Commentary is published, edited by Rev. Robert Goss, Rev. Mona West and Rev. Thomas Bohache.

of our youngest employees, Angel Collie, who is also our new representative on the Board of the LGBT Religious Archives, formerly associated with the Chicago Theological Seminary and now with the Pacific School of Religion. Our General Conferences in 2005 and 2007 were the largest in our history and we anticipate that same energy for July 2010 in Acapulco.

Friends, we are on the move and these are exciting times both for our local churches, who are deeply engaged in their communities, and for our global ministry, in which a generation of young, far-reaching spiritual activists are in training for and assuming leadership roles.

One might ask if we will go through periods of doubt and concern again. Of course we will—such is the nature of human institutions. In the past our response to difficulties has always been, "Be faithful!" and we have moved forward. That legacy will continue to serve us well.

Vivienne Hull in *Earth and Spirit* says: "Radical openness is the invocation of full-bodied living, of first-hand experience, being unafraid to immerse ourselves in the full drama of being alive at the cusp in history and to become participants in this great transitional moment as we move through the 21st century. It is not waiting to miss what's going on."

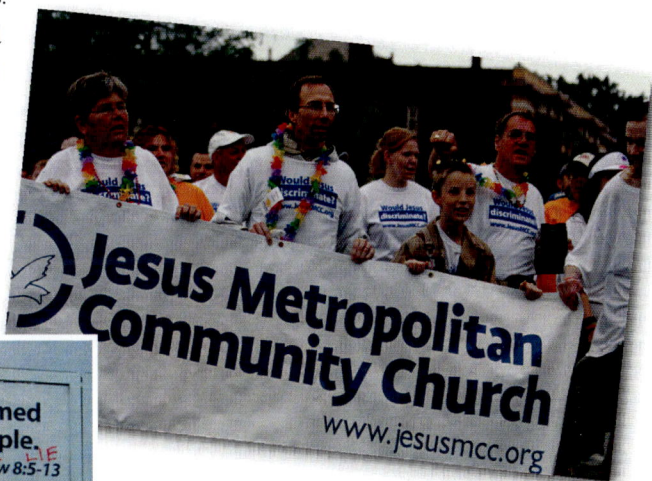

Various advertising and events in the *Would Jesus Discriminate?* campaign in Indianapolis.

July—In recognition of his long-time gay activism, and in particular his role in shaping the debate around same-sex marriage, the Governor General of Canada, Michaëlle Jean, appoints Rev. Dr. Brent Hawkes as a Member of the Order of Canada. His investiture will take place in February of 2008.

In partnership with Sunshine Cathedral MCC in Ft. Lauderdale, Florida, Christians in Jamaica establish an MCC congregation.

The film, *Call Me Troy*, which documents the life of Rev. Elder Perry and the founding of MCC is released by Tragoidia Moving Pictures.

The 2nd and 3rd phases of the *Would Jesus Discriminate?* Campaign are launched in Indianapolis; and the 1st phase is launched by All God's Children MCC in Minneapolis, Minnesota. The Campaign, to date, generates more media mentions of MCC than have occurred cumulatively in the organization's nearly 40-year history.

2007

General Conference XXIII July 2007 Scottsdale, Arizona
Theme: Building On Hope, Creating Our Future
Guest speakers include Jay Bakker, pastor of Revolution Church, son of Jim & Tammy Faye Bakker;
Peggy Campolo, member of the Council of Welcoming and Affirming Baptists;
Bishop Yvette Flunder, City of Refuge Community Church UCC;
Rev. Lynice Pinkard, family therapist and Program Development Specialist for the San Francisco Department of Public Health;
Donna Red Wing, Senior Advisor for Program & Development to the Interfaith Alliance in Washington, DC;
Bishop Carlton Pearson, Author, Speaker, Spiritual Leader, Recording Artist;
Marquis D. Hunt, founder of the Life Exchange.
Rev. Elder Don Eastman retires.
Delegates vote that General Conference will convene triennially, with the next event to be held in 2010 in Acapulco, Mexico.

We do not know all that tomorrow will bring, but we will not be waiting to miss what's going on. Until freedom is available to all, MCC and its people will be "on call" and ready to answer.

And all God's people say, "Amen."

A full circle—Rev. Troy Perry performed the first same-sex marriage on December 3, 1968 and has continued the fight for equal marriage rights ever since. Rev. Perry and his partner, Phillip Ray De Blieck, were married in Canada and filed suit in California for recognition of their marriage. The California Supreme Court ruled in favor of their suit in 2008, legalizing marriage for all.

Much of spiritual practice is just this:
cutting away what must be cut,
and letting remain what must remain.
Knowing what to cut—this is wisdom.
Being clear and strong enough
to make the cut when it is time for things
to go—this is courage.
Together, the practices of wisdom and courage
enable us, day by day and task by task,
to gradually simplify our life.

Wayne Muller in *How, Then, Shall We Live?*

Conference Anthems

Music can express the mystical experience better than language; it can tell of its mystery, joy, sadness, and peace far better than words can utter. The fatigued intellect finds a tonic and the harassed emotions find comfort in music.

Paul Brunton in *Meditations for People in Crisis.*

Free To Be — 1985 General Conference *Free to Be* Sacramento, California
(Marsha Stevens & Ken Caton)

Bridgebuilder — Rev. David Farrell's 10th anniversary at MCC San Diego
(Marsha Stevens & Ken Caton)

I Am Whole — 1986 SouthWest District Conference
(Marsha Stevens & LeRoy Dysart)

Perfect Love — 1987 General Conference *Perfect Love Casts Out All Fear* Miami Beach, Florida
(Marsha Stevens & Ken Caton)

Celebrate — 1988 MCC's 20th Anniversary Celebration, Los Angeles, California
(Marsha Stevens & Danny Ray)

Best Is Yet — 1988 MCC's 20th Anniversary Celebration Los Angeles, California
(Marsha Stevens & Danny Ray)

Good News — 1989 General Conference *Good News for All People* St. Paul, Minnesota
(Marsha Stevens & Ken Caton)

Open Door — 1991 General Conference *I Have Opened a Door* Phoenix, Arizona
(Marsha Stevens & Danny Ray)

Come Out And Go Forth — 1993 General Conference *For All the Nations* Phoenix, Arizona
(Marsha Stevens & Danny Ray)

Building Up One Another — 1994 Southwest District Conference
(Marsha Stevens & Ken Caton)

All Things Are Possible — 1995 General Conference *All Things are Possible* Atlanta, Georgia
(Marsha Stevens, Jane Syftestad & David Heid)

Pastor's Heart — (1996) Nancy Wilson's 10th Anniversary at MCC Los Angeles
(Marsha Stevens & LeRoy Dysart)

Light Of The World — 1997 General Conference *You are the Light of the World* Sydney, Australia
(Marsha Stevens & Chris Lobdell)

We Have Joy — 1999 General Conference *Jubilee of Joy* Los Angeles, California
(Marsha Stevens)

Adelante en Fe — 2001 General Conference *Moving Forward in Faith* Toronto, Ontario
(Marsha Stevens & the ICM Monterrey, Mexico church choir)

Let Your Light Shine — 2003 General Conference *Let Your Light Shine* Dallas, Texas
(Marsha Stevens-Pino, Glenna Shepherd and Cindy Stevens-Pino)

Future And A Hope — 2005 General Conference *A Future and a Hope* Calgary, Alberta
(Marsha Stevens-Pino & Chip Davis)

Built On Hope — 2007 General Conference *Building on Hope, Creating our Future* Scottsdale, Arizona
(Marsha Stevens-Pino)

MCC Firsts

1st service: *October 6, 1968 at the home of Rev. Troy Perry in Huntington Park, California.*

1st General Conference and formation the Universal Fellowship of Metropolitan Community Churches: *1970 in Los Angeles, California.*

1st classes held at Samaritan Bible Seminary: *September 1970.*

1st churches outside the US: *MCC of London (England, UK) and MCC Toronto (Ontario, Canada) in 1973.*

1st themed General Conference: *General Conference IV in Atlanta, Georgia; "Onward—As One"*

1st female clergy ordained & 1st female elected to Board of Elders: *Rev. Freda Smith in 1973.*

1st heterosexual clergy licensed: *Rev. June Norris in 1973.*

1st non-US clergy licensed: *Rev. Sylvanus Maduka of Nigeria in 1974.*

1st persons of color licensed as clergy: *Rev. Sylvanus Maduka (see above) and Rev. Jose Mojica in 1974.*

1st transgendered person licensed as clergy: *Rev. Heather (now Sky) Anderson in 1975.*

1st African-American licensed as clergy: *Rev. Delores (Dee) Jackson in Washington, D.C. in 1976.*

1st female pastor of the "Mother Church": *Rev. Jeri Ann Harvey, 1978.*

1st National March on Washington for Gay & Lesbian Rights (at which UFMCC sponsors worship services): *1979.*

1st non-US citizen elected as an Elder: *Rev. Jean White of London, England in 1979.*

1st person of color elected as an Elder: *Rev. Jeri Ann Harvey, a Native American, in 1979.*

1st responses to what will become the AIDS crisis: *1981.*

1st lay Elder elected: *Michael Mank in 1981.*

1st Asian clergy licensed: *Rev. Hong Tan in 1981.*

1st General Conference outside the USA: *General Conference XI in Toronto, Ontario, Canada in 1983.*

1st General Conference with equipment on-site to translate proceedings into Spanish: *General Conference XII in Sacramento, California in 1985.*

1st incidence of special programming for children at a General Conference: *General Conference XV in Phoenix, Arizona in 1991.*

1st transgendered person elected to the Board of Elders: *Rev. Willem (Bill) Hein, now Rev. Wilhelmina Hein, in 1991.*

1st District Conference held where English not the primary language: *Hamburg, Germany in 1992.*

1st African-American and Asian Elders: *Rev. Darlene Garner and Rev. Hong Tan in 1993.*

1st General Conference to offer (limited) virtual attendance: *General Conference XVIII in Sydney, New South Wales, Australia in 1997.*

1st non-elected Elder: *Rev. Jorge Sosa of Mexico City appointed to fill the unexpired term of Rev. Wilhelmina Hein, who resigned, in 1997.*

1st monthly cybercasts: *30-minute audio programs feature music, UFMCC musicians, and a message from Rev. Elder Perry in 1998.*

THE UFMCC TRANSITION TEAM

The following individuals served as the transition team for the restructuring plan adopted by the General Conference in 2001. Rev. Elder Don Eastman, Vice Moderator, served as Chair.

UFMCC Staff
Rev. Elder Don Eastman, Chair
Rev. Justin Tanis
Rev. Jim Birkitt
Ms. Margaret Mahlman
Mr. Charles Tigard, Staff to the team

Consultants
Rev. Arlene Ackerman
Ms. Wendy Foxworth
Rev. Marty Luna-Wolfe

Transition Advisory Group
Mr. Ken McLaughlin, Treasurer GLD
Mr. Gary Burns, Treasurer SCD
Rev. Judy Dahl, Global Outreach
Ms. Judy Dale, Great Lakes
Rev. Judy Davenport, Southeast
Ms. Cecilia Eggleston, European
Mr. Michael Ellard, Treasurer NWD
Mr. Bob Ewart, Treasurer SED
Rev. Diane Fisher, Eastern Canadian/Northeast
Rev. John Fowler, Australian
Mr. Ron Freeny, Treasurer SWD
Rev. Elder Darlene Garner, BOE
Elder CT Friesen
Rev. Dr. Brent Hawkes,
    Chair, Moderators' Nominating Committee
Elder Mel Johnson, BOE
Mr. Stan Kimer, COL
Ms. Peggy Lowell, Treasurer MAD,
Rev. Debbie Martin, Northwest
Rev. Jay Neely, Gulf Lower Atlantic
Rev. Ed Paul, South Central
Rev. Donald Pederson, Southwest
Rev. Elder Troy Perry, BOE
Rev. Ken Pilot, Mountains and Plains
Mr. Michael Price, Treasurer MAPD
Mr. Geoff Robbins, Treasurer ECD/NWD
Rev. Elder Nori Rost, BOE
Rev. Elder Hong Tan, BOE
Rev. Elder Nancy Wilson, BOE
Ms. Cassie Wylie, Treasurer GLAD

Region 1 Implementation Team
Ms. Susan Van Houten
Rev. David Pelletier
Mr. Peter Webster

Region 2 Implementation Team
Ms. Cassie Wylie
Rev. John Barbone
Rev. Dexter Brecht
Mr. Tom Merrill
Ms. Bobbi Powell

Region 3 Implementation Team
Rev. Candace Shultis
Ms Debbie Krusemark
Rev. Pablo Navarro

Region 4 Implementation Team
Rev. Thomas Friedhoff
Ms. Laurence Vergez
Mr. Timothy Spears
Ms. Sharon Cox
Rev. Paul Mokgethi
Ms. Janine Preesman

Region 5 Implementation Team
Ms. Joyce Robbins
Mr. Tom O'Laughlin
Rev. Mark Bidwell

Region 6 Implementation Team
Mr. Desmer Benson
Rev. Dan Koeshall
Ms. Velma Garcia
Mr. Joaquin Acosta
Ms. Julie Tizard

Region 7 Implementation Team
Rev. Paul Anway
Rev. Julia Seward
Rev. Jill Nelson
Rev. Wanda Floyd

Region 8 Implementation Team
Mr. David Sorey
Rev. Renae Phillips
Rev. Lillie Brock

BOARDS, COUNCIL AND STAFF

*The Team That Beats With One Heart***

Board of Elders
Moderator	Rev. Elder Nancy Wilson
Region 1	Rev. Elder Ken Martin
Region 2	Rev. Elder Jim Mitulski
Region 3	Rev. Elder Arlene Ackerman
Region 4	Rev. Elder Glenna Shepherd
Region 5	Rev. Elder Diane Fisher
Region 6	Rev. Elder Darlene Garner, Vice Moderator
Region 7	Rev. Elder Lillie Brock

Board of Administration
Marvin N. Bagwell
Barbara Crabtree
Julie Krueger
Rev. Jeff Miner
John Vespa
Marsha Warren

Lay Ministry Council
Bryan Parker
Marsha Stevens-Pino
Charlene Bisordi
Paul Johnstone
Jan Meils
Randi Williams

Executive Director
Rev. Dr. Cindi Love

Denominational Staff
Kathy Beasley*
Rev. Dr. Sharon Bezner
Florin Buhuceanu*
Jim Birkitt
Franklin Calvin*
Carlos Chavez
Ritchie Crownfield
Angel Collie
Judy Dale*
Tammy Erwin
Rev. Thomas Friedhoff*
Vickey Gibbs
Rev. Jennifer Glass*
Rev. Robert Griffin*
Rev. Hector Gutierrez*
Kay Hale
Capt. Katie Harris (Ret.)*
Bill Hooper
Jennifer Justice
Irma Bauer-Levesque
Joshua Love
Melanie Martinez
Connie Meadows*
Jason O'Neill
Valarie Parson*
Stedney Phillips
Joe Rattan*
Leah Sloan
Frank Zerilli*

Rev. Dr. Cindi Love concept/writer

Joseph Rattan concept/designer

Leah Sloan editor

Frank Zerilli archivist

Special thanks to all of you whose efforts to include as much information and as many persons as possible have made this 40th Anniversary book a reality. We regret any inaccuracies or omissions that may have occurred.

*not pictured

** MCC team members chose the name "The Team That Beats With One Heart" at the staff retreat in May 2006.

pictured above:

front row:
Bill Hooper, Jennifer Justice, Joshua Love, Sharon Bezner, Jim Mitulski

2nd row:
Darlene Garner, Stedney Phillips, Irma Bauer Levesque, Cindi Love, Kay Hale

3rd row:
Angel Collie, Glenna Shepherd, Melanie Martinez, Vickey Gibbs, Carlos Chavez, Lillie Brock

4th row:
Christy Ebner, Jim Birkitt, Leah Sloan, Diane Fisher, Steve Marlowe

back row:
Ritchie Crownfield, Jason O'Neill

Rev. Elder Ken Martin, Region 1

Rev. Elder Jim Mitulski, Region 2

Rev. Elder Arlene Ackerman, Region 3

Rev. Elder Glenna Shepherd, Region 4

Rev. Elder Diane Fisher, Region 5

Rev. Elder Darlene Garner, Region 6
Vice Moderator

Rev. Elder Lillie Brock, Region 7

PAST AND PRESENT ELDERS OF METROPOLITAN COMMUNITY CHURCHES

Rev. Elder Arlene Ackerman
2003-current

Rev. Elder Charlie Arehart
1976-1983; 1987-1991

Rev. Elder Roy Birchard
1974-1975

Rev. Elder Lillie Brock
2003-current

Rev. Elder Carol Cureton
1975-1979

Rev. Elder Don Eastman
1983-2007

Rev. Elder Cecilia Eggleston
2003-2007

Rev. Elder Diane Fisher
2003-current

Elder Clark Friesen
1997-2001

Rev. Elder Darlene Garner
1993-current

Rev. Elder John Gill
1973-1976

Rev. Elder Jeri Ann Harvey
1979-1987

Rev. Elder Wilhelmina Hein
1991-1996

Rev. Elder John H. Hose
1969-1981

Elder Mel Johnson
2001-2003

Rev. Elder Lou Loynes
1969-1973

Elder Michael Mank
1981-1987

Rev. Elder Debbie Martin
2003-2007

Rev. Elder Kenneth Martin
2007-current

Rev. Elder Jim Mitulski
2005-2008

Rev. Elder Troy D. Perry
1968-2005

Rev. Elder Richard Ploen
1969-1974

Elder Larry Rodriguez
1987-1997

Rev. Elder Nori Rost
1999-2003

Rev. Elder Armando Sanchez
2003-2005

Rev. Elder James Sandmire
1973-1979

Rev. Elder Glenna Shepherd
2007-current

Rev. Elder Freda Smith
1973-1993

Rev. Elder Jorge Sosa
1997-1999

Rev. Elder Gill Storey
2003-2006

Rev. Elder Hong Tan
1993-2003

Rev. Elder Richard Vincent
1973-1976

Rev. Elder Jean White
1979-1993

Rev. Elder Nancy L. Wilson
1976-2003; 2005-current

Universal Fellowship of Metropolitan Community Churches serves in the United States, Central & South America, Mexico, Canada, the Caribbean, Eastern & Western Europe, Malaysia, Philippines, Australia, New Zealand and Africa.

General Conference Offices in: Abilene, Atlanta, Austin, Boston, Dallas, Denver, Fort Lauderdale, Houston, Los Angeles, New York, Orlando, Portland, Provincetown, San Francisco, Sarasota, Bucharest, Cape Town, Guadalajara, Lancaster, London and Stuttgart.

Moderator Rev. Elder Nancy Wilson, Presiding
3293 Fruitville Road, No. 105, Sarasota, Florida 34237

Executive Director Rev. Dr. Cindi Love
1500 Industrial Boulevard, Suite 210, Abilene, Texas 79602

ISBN 142518283-6